madness, addiction & love

LILLY WHITE

◆ **FriesenPress**

Suite 300 - 990 Fort St
Victoria, BC, V8V 3K2
Canada

www.friesenpress.com

Copyright © 2016 by Lilly White / Whitelight
First Edition — 2016

Foreword: Andrew Harvey
Author Photos by Shawn De Salvo

All rights reserved.

No portion this book may be reproduced mechanically, electrically , or by any other means, including photocopying with our written permission of the author. It is illegal to copy this book, post it to a website, or distribute, it by any other means without permission from the author or publisher.

ISBN
978-1-4602-9339-3 (Hardcover)
978-1-4602-9340-9 (Paperback)
978-1-4602-9341-6 (eBook)

1. FAMILY & RELATIONSHIPS, FAMILY RELATIONSHIPS

Distributed to the trade by The Ingram Book Company

Table of Contents

Praise for *Madness, Addiction, and Love*. 1

Madness, Addiction & Love. 4

Passing on pain to the next generation 5

Upsetting family with truth 6

East Timor, May 2003 7

Foreword. 8

Introduction 9

Hurt people hurt people 10

Now is not the time to be afraid. .12

Mental illness—No one wants to talk about it 13

The Beginning 15

Death or a beating?. 19

Jesse, Mary, and all that is Horny, I mean Holy. 23

Shame or blame 25

Snow White 28

Another night of crazy Madness: Dougie, Sally, and Copp . .30

The freedom of wheels 33

The fairy meets her knight 34

Nuns & roses 37

We are transferred to Fredericton, NB, in 1975 40

The drunken labour. 41

The twin 44

The fairy falls off her pedestal. 46

1979: Crazy Nellie. Silly Lilly. 49

The sigh 53

An abundance of debt. 54

To kill or not to kill 56

The Grand of Grand Falls. Falling into Madness. 58

The Madness of ME. 62

Brushes with Spirit in Rexton 64

We are all given a wee bit of Madness. Use it wisely 66

Feb 1991: John arrives home weighed down. 69

Fredericton, Oct 7, 1991: A new beginning, bittersweet. 72

Journey into the Twelve Steps. 74

Beauty and the Beast 76

David who?. 78

Listen to your gut; your gut has a brain 80

Angels' grace, Amanda's gifts 83

I SURRENDER 85

Merciful God 87

The mole on our shoulders 89

The dark night of the soul. 91

Dark Night of My Soul. 94

Another example of Madness. 95

PATTERNS and Details 98

When we bring something into being we become
Co Creators with the Universe.. 100

SUCIDE is never the answer to, "how do we find balance?" 102

Remorse to Redemption. 107

Redemption To Forgiveness 110

A story, a Dance, the beginning of self-love 113

The hole in the floor. 115

Saboteur or Gambler? 2004 117

Bulgaria, Greece and Angels. 120

What we lost in the fire 124

Retail, not a fairy-tale	126
The most heart-wrenching decision I ever made	129
What in the name of all that is holy were you thinking?	133
"Power Up Your Life ," through grief of any kind.	136
The Code of Silence	138
What is this Love we all talk about?	141
Cruelty	142
The madness of lies, whys & ties	144
Love is an action word	148
How often throughout our day do we give thanks?	150
Blood, Stress and Fears	151
For the love of food and our addictions	153
What is gluten?	154
Modern grain vs. ancient grain	156
The brain drain	157
Nutrients	158
The probiotic + Caesarean link to gluten sensitivities	159
The consciousness piece	160
Ancient grain vs. modern grains	161
Einkorn	162
Protocol and pantry overhaul	164
The Heartbeat of A Marriage 2015	165
Isn't life grand?	168
Love	170
Despair - have you ever been in des-pair?	173
What do a few pages on despair have to do with the chapter in this book on love?	176
Silence is golden and you are worth your right to that gold. For love	177
A state of homelessness	179

Dying to be awake, Madness & Joy. 181
Evolve; get involved with your health. 184
St. Dymphna, ...186
You Are An Empowered Being Of Light. 188
The Challenge. 190
Ten Days Working with Your Mind. 191
Ten Days Working with Your Body 200
Ten Days Working with Your Spirit. 211
30-Day Challenge Workbook. 221
The Final Chapter 222
Acknowledgements. 226

Praise for *Madness, Addiction, and Love*

What a brave book you have written!
Madness, Addiction, and Love will take you to the depths of despair and back to joy. Like a kaleidoscope of shifting colors, you will look at Lilly's story and see echoes of your own. This is an unforgettable book about mental illness and its impact on several generations. There is much pain, but even more love in this work.
    - Lynne Klippel author of Overcomers, Inc.

Madness, Addiction, and Love is a brilliant description of real life madness and addiction. It nearly broke my heart at times and I suspect it will affect you the same way.
Yet, Lilly is so open and honest about her life that it was difficult to put her book down.
Hers is a unique story of the strength and endurance she found to cling on to life. Even in her darkest hours, she knew that her Angels, and the Divine, would see her through.
Congratulations Lilly.
    - Conrad Toner, Lifecoach

A courageous and poignant view into a life... a life deeply committed to love.
    - Carell Framer: Usui Reiki Master, Pachakuti Mesa Bundle Carrier, Visual Artist, Founding Director of Conscious Healing Institute, Grandmother.

Lilly White has written a book that is raw with pain, humor, and heart vulnerability. I highly recommend this book for its authenticity and insight. I plan to share it with my therapy clients.
- Deborah Owen-Sohocki, LPC

Madness Addiction and Love takes you on a journey through the life of a woman brave enough to share what most shouldn't have to survive. It is a story so raw yet rife with the kind of humor only Lilly could inject so eloquently onto such a brave excursion through madness, addiction and ultimately, love; a journey told, not in vain, but in service. One told bravely, with purpose, with soul and in the spirit of pulling someone else through the tribulations of madness and addiction that can only be solved and dissolved, with Love. Lilly travels a path, in this book and in life, of purpose, with such a reverence for life and a light so bright, you'd never know her past but to read it on these well lived pages. Her writing is a salve for the soul.
- Kerry Ford, Sovereign Health Practitioner, ww.panandpanacea.com

With an open heart and joy in her soul Lilly shows how to walk through human life facing our challenges and always maintaining wonder.
- Daniel Peralta, A fashionista/ Warrior from the soul of creativity.

This book captures the chaos of mental illness and addiction while demonstrating the power of love in the journey to healing. If you or someone you know struggles with bi-polar disorder, give them this book. Lilly does a fabulous job of demonstrating how chaos need not become the new normal and how patience, dialogue and understanding are the key to living well with mental illness.
- Dee-Anne Shepard/ Nurse Practitioner with specialty in mental Health.

There are many things that touched me directly within *Madness, Addiction & Love*. Lilly White has written a book that few could write. Speaking from her heart and soul, it reached mine. Her loving spirit and the pain she went through in her growth. Trials that we all go through in some way within our lives. All who read this book will benefit. Anyone who has someone in their life that suffers from mental illness, addiction and/or loss will truly feel her experiences in some way. In reading this book, I came away with the feeling that I was not alone, and that there was truly hope. Hope for us all. Lilly is guided by spirit, and speaks with truth, I knew that from her last book "365 Ways to Power Up Your Life." This book strongly confirmed what I believe and that is Lilly White is providing light and love for us in our darkest times.

I feel honored and blessed to know Lilly… May God forever bless – always.

- Amy C. Moore, Spiritual Director, Archetype Consultant. Facebook: Mystics Without Monasteries – Dark Night of the Soul.

Madness, Addiction & Love

For our daughters, Melanie and Amanda, our grandchildren, and the generations to follow—I adore you. Amanda you continue to inspire me.

For my siblings —I love you.

For John—My life is Mad and Addictive, and you love me anyway.

Melanie—May you rest in peace my darling and know your death will not be in vain. You have made a difference for your children and their babies yet to be born.

To my Parents, thank you for raising us the best way you knew, given the tools you were given. There is no fault, only forgiveness & love. Rest now.

To friends, too many to mention. Thank you for not taking things personally when I was in the dark night. You know who you are.

To Caroline Myss, my teacher, the student was ready.

To Andrew Harvey. In 2011 you gave me Hope. You breathe a light into me and planted a seed.

I am now giving birth to that.

Passing on pain to the next generation

Why are children always first to feel the pain and why do they hurt the worst? Somehow it doesn't seem right. Every time I cried, I knew I was hurting my children.

That hurt carries on to their children.

When a child, a brother, a friend, takes his or her life, a future dies with them. Be it theirs or our own. Nothing is ever the same. Those left behind take another path, usually one they have not taken before. Grief can be a catalyst for change.

When we are able to take responsibility for what is ours, not with guilt or blame, but as part and parcel of a family, healing can begin.

Upsetting family with truth

Someone had mentioned to me that our dad would be upset about my writings. Actually, he called me a ^A$(@_up fairy. Everyone needs an outlet. His truth is his truth. I will not judge him. I will discuss these writings with Dad. I started them in 2003 when I was in East Timor, but I knew that one of my parents would have to be gone before they were published. Truth is truth—not to hurt, but to help future generations.

How do we help future generations when we live in denial? How will our grandchildren blossom and serve when they do not know where they came from?

No excellent soul is exempt from a mixture of madness.

Aristotle

In the course of the year, a combat takes place between the forces of light and the forces of darkness, eventuating in the revolution of the seasons. Human beings master these changes in nature by noting their regularity and marking off the passage of time accordingly. In this way, order and clarity appear in the apparently chaotic changes of the seasons, and human beings are able to adjust themselves in advance to the demands of the different times.

The *I Ching*

East Timor, May 2003

It appears it is time,
I know I can rhyme,
I have had this story for years.
Why all the fears?
They have spilled into tears,
this story I now have to tell.
It is all very simple, spiritually for those of us who have been to hell.
No, it is not that dramatic,
but why do I panic
as soon as I start to remember?
It is so long ago,
I am still not that old.
But remember I must,
for in God I do trust,
and his lessons have turned into gold.

Foreword

Sometimes a grave is not for bodies. It can be for the soul; the tomb of our fate. That forbidding, fateful soul contract.

For most of my life I have had weighty concerns and fears of living in madness, addiction, and love. I either had too much or not enough of all three. I'd hear, "I love you," then be beaten within a second of my next breath. I was on pins and needles constantly. Survival became a daily prayer.

By thirteen I was on booze. By thirty-six I was on my knees begging to a higher power to help me end it all. That day was October 7, 1991. I had no idea how that prayer was going to be answered. I was about to find out what real madness is, learn about addiction, find love through letting go… and finally through death.

You are about to take a wild journey with me. Hang on—you will laugh out loud, hold your breath, and allow tears to flow. You will come to know that no matter what life throws at us, we are all whole—holy.

There is a wee bit of madness, addiction, and love in each of us. Mental illness is difficult to talk about, let alone to own up to. My hope is that as you read this you see for yourself that we are normal people; the folks next door. Our addictions can be tamed. We are usually creative, loving, and wise. We may have walked in despair, but we have found the road to hope. Our journeys may be yours. If that is the case, know that you are not alone.

Introduction

This book is a memoir, written in three parts. Part One describes the madness I lived in, from birth and into my late thirties, until I entered a twelve-step program. Part Two tells of the addictions I felt after I stopped drinking, and of the addiction of others. Part Three is about how to escape this affliction through all that is real. Love.

It is about mental illness; living with someone mentally ill; birthing mental illness; burying mental illness and hiding it in a closet—the closet of our own minds.

It is written with hope. Hope that we may embrace this suffering with grace instead of fear. We cannot heal what we do not acknowledge.

We think mental illness belongs in an institution. We think it will not affect us because we live on the outside. Look around you. It's in your work place and on the road driving while you are travelling. It's sitting next to you in the restaurant where you are dining. Maybe you are sleeping next to someone ill, or maybe a close relative has shut him or herself out of your life. It's everywhere, and it's time we stopped being afraid; we need to be brave and aware.

Hurt people hurt people

I first heard this phrase when I entered a twelve-step program in 1991. It changed me.

I remember having a dream not long after I heard this. In the dream, I was on a bus, on my way to jail for something I had not done. Everyone—friends, family, husband John—was pointing their fingers at me in judgment. I was holding a baby in my arms as the bus was driving away. I did not care what anyone else thought of me. Spirit knew I had not done anything wrong, and that was all that mattered. I awoke knowing that if I lived my life as such, between myself and the God of my understanding, I would be safe. It would not matter what anyone thought of me or how he or she judged my actions.

I have never intentionally said or done anything to cause harm, except on Mothers' Day 2014. Then, I hurt and I wanted to hurt.

It is interesting to witness the fear rise up in me regarding this book, *Madness, Addiction & Love*. I do not know why I am guided to tell my story. Only that I must if Mental Illness is to be accepted in our family.

I began this book in 2003 while visiting East Timor with my husband John, who was on a United Nations mission there. At the time, this book had a different name (*An Autobiography in Rhyme*). In Timor, I witnessed the aftermath of war. This war was fought with guns and machetes. It was the children who were paying the price. Our family wars are no different. They are fought with words and abandonment. Once again it is the children who suffer, and their children, if we do not break the patterns.

War of any kind is madness. Power is an addiction. Love is the only antidote.

Freeing myself from the pain of the backlash from family and friends will not be easy, but I will allow spirit to have me. I will my will to speak up so that mental illness is not seen or understood as an affliction we put upon ourselves. Instead, it is a combination of many things: our culture, the food we eat, the misunderstanding of how we are wired, our DNA.

As you read through these pages, allow spirit to guide you. We must learn not to take ourselves so seriously—it only hurts our hearts. Take what you need; leave the rest.

Now is not the time to be afraid

Now is not the time to be afraid. Be aware. We stand in unison as a collective. We stand in love and courage and will soldier on, no matter what is thrown at us. This is our world. This chaos is happening everywhere; in our mind/bodies, in our homes, our towns, our countries, our planet. Breathe, continue to be in your light, pass that light on and together we will brighten the darkness.

"For today, let the spirit of light have us." What does that mean? Allow your attention to be in prayer. Pray all day long if you have to. That does not mean we need to be in meditation, on our knees, or in a church. Your mind/body is your church. If you choose to be on your knees, go for it. Continue to be in gratitude for the small things; the sun, your children, your health, your day. You are alive at this moment. Make the most of it. Help where needed, pray for the families involved in today's terror in Ottawa. Pray for the soldier and his family in Quebec, the soldier here in Ottawa. All is in Divine order. Difficult to believe, I realize, but nothing is random. Your prayers do make a difference; it is part of your sacred contract. Remember what you came here for. Do not allow the darkness to shadow your light. Be YOU, you beautiful being of Light.

Inhale now. The world is changing and we are called to be a part of that transformation.

Mental illness—No one wants to talk about it

Have you ever been around someone who is angry?

You are aware they are in grief, over the loss of someone or something; a job, a house, a dream. Do you run from them? Do you set your boundaries and leave? Boundaries are great to have, but I can see how boundaries can be a form of running. People run from those who are in anger. I can understand, but perhaps there is another soul lesson here.

While watching the news (on August 26, 2015), I saw another shooting, this time in Roanoke, Virginia. Two young lives were taken quickly by an angry, disgruntled individual who murdered his victims on live TV. His anger had shown over the years, in many ways. In his rage and anger, his answer was, "Hey, I'll fix you."

Mental illness is what needs to be addressed, not gun control. Guns are not the issue. People and the mental illness they live in—that is the problem. No one is addressing that subject. Are we too afraid we may see ourselves?

Why are we so afraid of saying and admitting we are ill? Why are we afraid of talking about mental illness? Mental illness is not only about schizophrenia or depression. Look around at us. Do you know someone who is drinking daily for no reason? Maybe someone is eating compulsively, and then dieting repeatedly? Or spending money on items they do not need and going into debt? Maybe they need to always be right?

Who among us is power hungry, raging constantly, attention-seeking, working incessantly, or working-out relentlessly? Are you witnessing friends drugging themselves and then hiding for a few days? Perhaps you know people who have smoked until they became ill, and still refuse to quit.

Mental illness is not only for those who need to be put away. It is all around us; in front of us, next to us, behind us, in us.

For the love of God, let's wake up! Let's talk about it. Mental is not a mute word. It is part of our core, our wholeness. We and our society have become splintered. It is time to repair ourselves and help one another. Stop hiding. Open up. Love one another. Pray together. Play together. There is always HOPE (help others, pray, play everyway), but not if we are afraid of being ill. Bring the boogeyman out in the center and have compassion for this energy. Learn to embrace and love it. Only then can we heal it.

The Beginning

There are many reasons, factors, and elements for our mental states.

Where and when did mine start? I was born in Stephenville, Newfoundland. Newfoundland is an island on the east coast of Canada. The last province to join Confederation (1949). It was a 51-49 split vote. An interesting coincidence, as for most of my life that was how I lived; in between light and shadow, a 51-49 balance. The 51% was the shadow.

My parents lived out their lives and love for one another by borrowing from their tomorrows. Socializing, debts, and drinking became a way of life. They worked hard, and by 1960 there were five children to raise. Their idea of survival was a roof over our heads, food, and a position in society; what anyone living in the 1950s-60s would have wanted. It was the unhealthiest of times.

As a child, fear was always a part of my being; fear of spirits I could not see; fear of evil unknown to me; fear of anger, of not being enough. Fear of failure to please. Fear of the unknown and disease. Ever since I could remember, it was "love me now, love me tender." God forbid, I would surrender. Surrender to the light of day, it did help the fear to go away.

Throughout those days of self-deceit, thank God for grandparents! I worshipped them both and lay at their feet. I would visit them often, afraid to go home; the anger on Ocean Drive and living with my parents was toxic, so my heart and I would roam…to my grandparents, to my uncles and aunts…

Altogether, I stayed with my grandparents in Point aux Mal for twelve years. Whenever I returned home, it was in tears. It began when I was nine months old and my mother was admitted into hospital for almost a year with tuberculosis. If I'd had my way I would have never left Point aux Mal, but life was not a dream…you did not do as you pleased or have it all.

At the tender age of twelve, time stood still—Grandma's time was up. It was spring, but I could not hear a bird sing; my heart was bleeding, I felt the sting. The woman I had come to adore—Anastasia—in her coffin, looked calm, at peace, almost bored. This love I felt, this safe haven—how could she leave me? In that little body of twelve, those questions I asked. No answers were heard.

I built a wall. One of deceit—no one must know or they will leave. I'll pretend I am strong. I'll act out my part. This life is not easy but hey, this is me—I am smart.

At about this time the mask was found. No one was watching—they were not around. For many a year this mask was worn, not removed until my late thirties, when my body and soul were torn.

The days from twelve to seventeen years of age are hazy…

One thing I wasn't, and that was lazy. School, work, family, boys, dancing, drumming, driving motorcycles, toys…

My fears were so huge that I couldn't learn, so school was a write-off. It was never my turn. I'd struggle and fail, start over again; I repeated grades three and ten, and the shame of that still lights from within. I was told I had an above average IQ, but because I could not spell, I thought I was stupid.

Working in the dress shop that my mother owned was rewarding, fun, and creative, and I had energy to burn.

I still love to sell, and that we did.
It was Rosemary's Dress Shop; nothing was hid.
Working there weekly taught me much—
I loved the smell of the fabric, the magic, the touch.

Working with my mother created a bond;
she was more of a friend, not just my mom.
A love we had, a mutual respect,
but I have to tell you sometimes it felt like a test.

I would stand up to anyone who threatened my need,
my belief in myself, my ego to feed.
Being so young, wilful, and naïve,
it wasn't long I began to suffer from the "Disease to Please."

I would stand up to anyone who threatened my need to be myself. My father would yell, time and again. It did not matter, I'd stand up and ask for more—the fear would still be there; the proof the urine, all on the floor. I'd protect my siblings, lie, and steal—he would always know, and the belt I would feel.

There were days of sunshine, rain, and thunder,
and when I look back I begin to wonder.
I stepped away from the pain,
for to keep it brought no gain.
It's over now, it means very little.
It gave me the tools to be strong, not brittle.

The years were filled with wonder—
discovering myself, living like thunder.
I smoked, I danced, a few drugs I did try—
Each time I got caught…darn it, I'd lie.

Even though I was afraid of my father, he did help me experience a little freedom. It came in the form of a motorbike.

It rode like a dream.
This Honda, and me,
we were quite a team!

With blue suede boots and a jacket to match,
I did not know it then, but for any young man I'd be quite a catch.

Those were the best memories for me as a teen—
I'd laugh and I'd cry but it was my machine.

The breeze, the speed on the road,
escaping into freedom that became my code.

Out on the road I was me, I was me.
I drove like a speed diva; on the road I was free.
Then it happened, an accident I did have;
the bike it tipped over and I burnt my right calf.
The reality set in, I was careless and young.
I gave the bike to my brother, sad; my face, oh how it hung.

There are a few days in these years that I would like to share with you, so you can come to an understanding of what mental illness looks and feels like. It was only in 2013, after the death of my mother, that I came to the realization that she drank because she had married someone who was bipolar. Dad was never diagnosed, but as you read through these pages you will understand the behaviour. Our daughter Melanie was diagnosed with personality disorder while living with us (in 1995), and then in 2008 with bipolar disorder. I know the behaviours only too well.

Both my parents were alcoholics. Part of my story, when I entered an AA program in 1991, was that I had never seen my father drunk, but I'd seldom seen him without a drink. When he was not drinking, he was in a rage. Just the opposite of what would be considered an alcoholic. When he was NOT drinking, I was in FEAR.

In the next few chapters, we will enter into my life as a teenager. My aim is not to scare you about what your child is up to, but to make you aware that madness and addiction can start early. For me, the lying to my father became an addiction based on his madness. Sometimes it did not work, but the addiction to lying to save myself became my madness.

As I grew into adulthood, my mantra soon became, "Be aware, not afraid."

Death or a beating?

Death or a beating? My choice. Not much of a choice, but fear I had and it was big—silly me I always hid. This is a memory; a beginning of my crazies. Both our father's and mine.

It was February 1971. My friend Karen and I wanted to go to Port aux Basques for a K-20 weekend filled with meetings and a dance. K-20 is a branch of the Kinsmen for teenagers (ages thirteen to twenty). I could go on two conditions: first, we had to go with a Kinsman and Kinette who would chaperone us; second, I was not allowed to stay at the hotel like everyone else. I had to stay with a friend.

The day before we were to leave, I received a phone call from the friend I was to stay with—her granny had died.

I'll stay at a hotel; I just won't let my parents know. That is part of the madness: lie. You'll always get caught, but lie anyway. I was going to be in trouble in any case, so what did it matter?

I remember the Port aux Basques drive with Corinne and Jim like it was yesterday. They were my friends and I loved them. They were good friends with my folks, but they were young and cool; you could talk with them about anything. They did not have children of their own, and the kids from K-20 were special to them.

We checked into the hotel, went to dinner as a group, and turned in early. Saturday there were meetings all day. Evening drew near—Party-dance time.

I cannot remember how it happened; I only remember being out on the fire escape with friends, drinking (of course) and the next thing we heard was, "HEEEELP!" One of our K-20 friends had just fallen off the fire escape. By the grace of God and all that is holy, she was alive. An ambulance arrived and all four of us drove with her to the hospital and waited out the long night as doctors mended her. She was pretty banged up, plus had a broken arm. Lucky girl.

Early Sunday we packed up our bags, along with our hangovers, and left for the long, three to four-hour drive home. (That is how long it took in the early seventies—now you can drive it in two.) During the drive, I was trying to find a way to tell my father the truth about where I had stayed and why. There would be hell to pay. I was scared, so I was not in a hurry for that drive to end. When we turned onto Ocean Drive I was saved. There was a car in the driveway. Yippee! We had company!

Remember, part of my story when I was living at home is that when my father was not drinking he was in a rage, and when he drank he was happy and calm (not your usual alcoholic).

When I entered, he was happy and calm, enjoying his company, Kevin H. "There you are," he said. "How was your weekend?"

"Great," I replied. I excused myself and went to my room. Even then that room had magic. Today I would call it my sacred space. Mom had decorated it in blue, white, and red. I loved that little room of bliss, especially when it was my own room, after our housekeepers left. (That's another chapter.)

All was fine and dandy, or so, once again, I believed...*Jesus, I cannot get away with anything!* Monday evening Mom returned home from where? You guessed it, a Kinette meeting. I had not bothered to tell Corinne that I would be keeping where we stayed a secret. I was sure it would not come up—they would not have talked about it in such detail if that crazy bitch friend of ours had not fallen off the fire escape.

Mom entered the room, waking me from a hell-free dream, with, "Lillian, if you do not tell your father the truth, I will...and you know what will happen." What was she talking about? It was going to happen no matter what. I was in deep. Again.

The next day I slowly dressed for school, which was just next to the cliff overlooking St. George's Bay (you could actually see St. Stephen's school and church from our home). I was sick in my gut, in my head, in my heart.

What am I to do now? I was not thinking and not caring any more. I did not want any more days like before; punishments were brutal. At lunch hour, I purchased a bottle of aspirin and sat on the banks overlooking the bay, staring outwards to Harmon Air Force Base. There is a cliff that you are able to see in the near distance. It was always a welcoming sight when we used to fly into Stephenville. There is no other view in the world like that hypnotic sight. I stared at it for the longest time as I swallowed the entire contents of the aspirin bottle. I was not sure what would happen, but I hoped it was fast. An hour went by—nothing. All I had was a pain in the gut. (No wonder I had ulcers and was hospitalized for them a few years later.) Gee, do you think it might have anything to do with being stupid and scared?

By four p.m. I knew I could not go home. I walked past Dad's store…slowly… *No, I cannot go in.* I walked past Mom's store…*No, she is a blabbermouth.*

I know—I will go talk to a priest.

I rang the big doorbell. Father Something-or-other told me he was too busy to discuss such foolishness. The door slammed shut.

Oh well, there are the nuns. I just hoped that whoever opened the door was not one of my teachers—especially not Sister Rosalie. My prayer was answered: I did not know this Sister. She was young, smiling (something Rosalie knew nothing about). She invited me in. I discussed with her my fear, and we talked for a long time. She suggested I go home and tell the truth; that my father would understand. I felt hope for the first time in my life. I felt like I felt when I'd had that first drink of sloe gin and 7; comforted, warm, safe.

I did not take West Street to walk home; I decided to take the walk by the beloved cliff overlooking the bay. I walked into the field and up Ocean Drive.

Sister Irene thought she was doing the right thing by calling my father to explain the situation while I took that walk home. When I entered through that door, I was thrown up against the wall and beaten so badly that my dad took me to the hospital. By this time, he was crying.

I was stunned into silence. I was confused once again. At the hospital, doctors fixed the wound on my arm. It wasn't that bad—we had thought it was broken. It was not. Only bleeding. We went home, and back in my room, Dad began to ask questions again. I couldn't speak. I was too numb.

Plus, I had taken a bottle of aspirin that afternoon and felt sick—I had mentioned that to the doctor. He just shook his head.

My mother came into my bedroom just after Dad left and told me she did not believe I had taken the pills or she would have beaten me herself. It was not like my mother to say something like that, so once again the feeling that came over me was shame. Mom was leaving my room as I heard the front door open. A friend of theirs, my godmother Emma, was visiting. I heard Mom and Dad talking to her as if all was fine. Life was normal. I was relieved to hear Emma's voice, as I knew I would be left alone until the next day.

I went to sleep with a feeling of dread, heaviness, anxiety, and repulsion for myself. I was a mere sixteen years old, but I felt like an old woman.

Jesse, Mary, and all that is Horny, I mean Holy.

In 1994 I was following the AA program and in the care of a wonderful life coach/social worker. One day, Carolyn said to me: "Lil, you sound like someone who has been sexually abused."

"Carolyn, I have been abused in many ways, but the one thing I am absolutely sure of is that I was never sexually abused as a child…I do however remember showing my brother Derek what to do when we were around five and seven."

"Who showed you?" she asked.

"Well, I always heard both my grandparents and my parents having sex. My parents' room was next to mine, and when I was with my grandparents, I slept in their bedroom. It was a big room and I was on the other side of the room, but I always heard them. For some unknown reason to me at the time, I always knew what they were doing. One day, Gram held my doll on her knee and said, "Look what Grandpa gave me." I knew what she was talking about even though I was only nine.

(It is actually lovely to know, as I write this, that age was not a factor in their lovemaking.)

My real sex education came from a book my father owned that I took out of his room. I was fifteen at the time. *The Happy Hooker* and I spent twenty-four hours together; I read it from cover to cover in a day. I can recite every chapter to you even now, it had such an impact on me. An awakening.

I had been purchasing my dad's porn magazines since around the age of twelve. I would walk to AV Gallant's store, buy an ice cream, Dad's smokes and the magazine, and walk home slowly as I peeked through the contents. It was all normal back then. Porn was not covered in plastic wrap as it is today—remember this is almost fifty years ago.

It's strange that when I was young being around all this sex seemed normal. No one talked about sex much, but the silence, the silent secret, was normal. It was like a dark shadow that hung around my neck; everyone was doing it yet sex was forbidden. Double messages. That in itself drives us to madness.

When we tried to talk about it in the schools, it was "unholy." We were all horny—that's only normal, pre-teens and all, but we were longing to know more; the secret.

Jesse was a cutie and he and my friend Mary began dating at fourteen. By the time they were sixteen, they were having a baby. Mary left—went away so no knew, and the effects of that still haunt them today.

Now that I look back, I had an advantage—*The Happy Hooker* and Dad's mags. I did not need to experiment. Of course, now I see the insanity of thinking it was okay for your child to purchase your porn. Today he would be arrested.

Shame or blame

I remember when I was studying with Dr. Mario Martinez in 2005, the one lesson that I walked away with was this: "We are born with one of three wounds—shame, betrayal, abandonment."

Mine, of course, is shame.

There is one day that I want to share with you, simply to show you the mask—the madness we create inside ourselves when we are raised by mental illness.

I was thirteen years old. I had started my monthlies (my period) just after my grandmother died. She died in May of 1968, so I would have been thirteen years old. I considered myself a teenager. I was crazy in love with some boy or other. Doug, Carl, flavour of the month. Hey, we were kids, and hormones were running even at twelve. At St. Stephen's gym, there were weekly dances. It was a happening, happy place. I only now realize just how blessed we were. The gym hosted our cheerleading, the boys' basketball, our dances, and so much more. The teachers were working day and night.

One of these teachers was taking us on a bus outing. I believe it was our last week before school closed, and the teachers and bus driver were taking us to Barachois Pond Provincial Park for a swim and picnic. It is a beautiful large park—one of the most popular parks around the west coast of Newfoundland. My parents took us there every weekend for many years. For them it was a drinking party—for us kids it was free time away from them.

Anyhow, back to this one-day. The night before the school was to take us, I was in trouble again for something I cannot remember. I was brought into the kitchen; a kitchen of black and white tiles. I needed to be made an example of, so my siblings were told to come in. My pants were pulled down, and oh my GAWD, my pad fell to the floor. Blood everywhere. My father's rage was so wild, he did not even notice, thank God. All he could focus on was that God-awful black belt. (I do not mean judo here.) That black belt was pulled from his trousers more than my siblings and I care to remember. What we will always recollect is the snap of the buckle when it hit the floor or our buttocks. I did not feel shame that evening. This was just another show of force in a home where a king exercised his power on his servants.

The next day, however, I was so filled with shame. I was afraid that someone would find out or someone already knew that my pad had fallen off. That I had been bad and that I had been beaten down once again. By the time I was twelve or thirteen I was getting tired of it, and I suppose with the hormones kicking in I was also getting angrier; standing up more for myself, only to be broken down. One thing I know for sure, I always stood up to him. I would sass Dad back, try and rescue my mother or siblings, and get more. For some reason I did not care. "Beat me all you want. Leave them alone." That was my motto. I am sure my siblings who are old enough to remember can attest to that.

But this day, this one-day—the shame. Maybe it came from growing up, that feeling that you are not good enough. Especially me, it seems that no matter what I did, it must have been evil, incorrect, or ruthless, for I was always getting punished.

As we entered the bus, the teacher was smiling at me and I just knew she knew. I knew she felt sorry for me. I felt it all through my body. Maybe it was the way I was carrying myself. Maybe she could see my monthly pad or maybe it was the bruises. I got on that bus, and I sat way in the back. Not my usual style—I was typically with my friends; Marina, Maria, Betty. The gang.

We had an hour's drive so I went into a deep sleep. When I woke, I remember thinking to myself; *I do not have to be me today. I can pretend I am okay and I am happy.* I put on a mask and by the time we arrived I jumped happily off that bus and left the old me in the back, still sleeping.

During the day, my friends and I were teenagers—happily swimming, eating hotdogs, giggling at boys. A perfect day. We boarded the bus around four p.m. for our return to Stephenville. It was still sunny when we arrived home from the forty-five-minute drive. We parked in the parking lot, and as we left the bus, I removed my mask. I told my friends I wouldn't walk home with them on West Street but would take the beach cliff home.

Once again I was thinking about jumping over the cliff into the blackness of the Atlantic Ocean. I could not bear to return to that household. I could see our home from where I was standing. What could I expect upon entering the front door? That tiny space that had a small closet for all eight of us?

As I was standing there, a feeling came over me. While we were on our trip, a friend of mine had given me a small sample vial of perfume. Her mother was a rep for Avon, and Gloria had a small stash. I pulled the perfume from my pocket. The fragrance smothered me with pleasure. For a moment in time my fear was gone. I knew, I just knew, that if I jumped I would miss out on my future. I chose hope and walked slowly home, feeling lifted. By the time I entered the house, Dad was out at a meeting and the rest of the family was eating around the table. All was well.

(Interestingly enough, I worked for Crabtree & Evelyn, a perfume company, for twelve years, between the ages of forty and fifty-two. Some of the best memories in my life.)

Snow White

April 22, 1972, began like any ordinary day. Cold snow up to our arses in Stephenville.

I was overly excited; my girlfriend from Corner Brook was visiting for the weekend. Valerie Snow, Karen, and I had plans to go to another K-20 dance.

Valerie arrived at noon. We were in my bedroom and she had a terrible headache, so I gave her a few aspirin. We wanted her in tiptop shape for the dance!

Valerie was soon feeling better, so we met up with Karen at my mother's dress shop, went to the Sun Luck for Chinese, and arrived at the dance for nine p.m. My parents were chaperones; I had no problem with that.

We were all scattered on the dance floor when I was literally pulled off the floor by a friend of my dad's. His face was white as snow and I was in deep fear. What had happened? Was I going to be punished for something I did, which I did not do? As usual, my bladder went weak—it always did when I was in fear.

I was brought into a room. My parents were there, plus a few of their friends, and I could tell by the look on Dad's face that, yup, I did something again that I had not done. *Fudge. Again. Here we go.*

"What drugs are you and your friends on?"

As you read this I need you to know that if I say I did drugs in my lifetime four or five times, that is an overstatement. Drugs were not my gig—booze was.

I swore to them, no drugs. Because my parents were chaperoning, we had not even bothered to steal any of their booze that night. We were stone sober.

Valerie was stone dead.

I went weak—peed myself. "What do you mean she has died?"

Yes, they tell me, while on the dance floor, she collapsed into a heap.

We were brought home, Karen and me. We were in my room—stunned, confused. We heard crying coming through the front door. It was Valerie's mom. Her daughter, seventeen years of age, our beloved friend, has died of a brain aneurysm.

A few days later, friends in the K-20 and I take the drive to Corner Brook for her funeral. "Please tell me why there is fun in funeral?" I asked.

Our friend Joe, who was driving, said, "Oh Lillian, you think too much."

Yes, perhaps he was right. I thought too much, but I was tired of being told by my parents to stop crying. Why did I always have to be brave? They had suggested I not cry in front of Valerie's parents, as that would upset them more. So I put on another mask. One of courage.

I sang at the ceremony. Cat Stevens' song, "Morning Has Broken." Everyone else was crying, but not me. (Even today, all these years later, whenever I hear that song, a feeling of "suck it in" comes over me.)

Over the next year, my friends and I travelled back and forth to Corner Brook for meetings with K-20. Usually I ended up drinking and my friends and I stayed the night at Valerie's parents in Curling, a small suburb outside Corner Brook. When her mother entered our room at night, she sat on our bed and cried herself to sleep with us. It was during these times I allowed myself to cry. I am not sure if it was the drink spilling out of me and crying, or the pouring out of my heart.

It was only years later, when I was in my fifties, that Valerie's spirit visited me while I was driving.

It was May 2011. One of our granddaughters had just been born and I was driving home from the hospital. The spirit of Valerie and I laughed and called ourselves Snow White. Our last names. If this was crazy mad, so be it. I was comforted by her presence.

Another night of crazy Madness: Dougie, Sally, and Copp

It was December 23, 1971. Dad's birthday. It was a joke in our home that Mom always had a surprise birthday party for Dad. Every year, right up until the year she let spirit have her.

I had just turned sixteen that November, and for my birthday, Dad gave me a set of drums. Someone had come into his sporting goods store that did not have money to purchase a rifle for hunting season, but had something to trade. At the time, I had a pair of drumsticks, and every table in our home was beaten down around the edges from me trying to teach myself how to drum. I loved it, so you can imagine my excitement when I saw those babies sitting in our basement. I had a boyfriend, Doug, who drummed, and I was smitten—with him and with the beat. My nickname for those drums was "Dougie."

Anyway, this night of Dad's party I was having a great time. A friend of my parents, let's call her "Sally," and I shared more than we should have for my age. She confided things to me that no one so young should hear, but I had grown up fast in that household so we easily became good friends. I sat on the stairs with her, watching everyone having a good time; drinking, dancing…and she started giving me Sloe gin and 7 to drink. Jesus, Mary, and all that is holy, that was soooooome drink. I loved it! I drank, chatted, yakked. Out of the blue, Daddy-o asked me if I would play a set for his guest on my beloved Dougie.

You betcha! I was having the time of my life! When I finished my set, I politely went over to Daddy-o, sat on his knee, and wished him a happy birthday. He was telling me how proud of me he was when—YUCK,

YUCK, YUCK—I threw up all over him. (I should use the word vomit, but that would not be visual enough.) I threw up, out, over, and under him. It was one hell of a mess.

Now that you know my father, you are aware that Mother, myself, my siblings, and most of Stephenville were scared shitless of him and his rage. I am sure his friends were in a state of wonder and shock when they saw this unfolding. I was too drunk to remember how they reacted, but I remember his reaction. I am not sure if his head hit the ceiling first or my ass hit the wall faster. I was kicked upstairs to the bathroom with my mother and one of her friends (not Sally, she was hiding). Mom kept asking me where I got the drugs. I tried to tell her I was not on drugs, but I could not tell her I was drunk, for then I would have to tell where I got the booze. That was a secret between Sally and me. After my head was pulled from the toilet (I laugh as I write this), I was pushed into the car. Dad was taking me to the RCMP. No daughter of his was going to be on drugs and not go to jail for it.

Everything was blurry... but I remember the police officer—actually his last name was Copp; some of you from Stephenville who are reading this will remember him. He told Dad to take me home, as I was not on drugs. Dad could not smell the booze, because he was drinking. Why Copp did not lock both of us up is madness, now that I think of it. Anyway, no police cell for Lilly that night, so Dad proceeded to take me to the hospital. He had convinced himself I was a drug addict. I was not going to tell him it was Sally who gave me the drinks. (In fact, ten years later, when he was visiting us, he asked and I still would not betray her or ruin their friendship.)

At the hospital, the doctor was very concerned for me and told Dad to take me home. "She is not on drugs." He told Dad that someone must have slipped me a mickey.

Oh Doctor, thank you Doctor, I think I love you! You have just saved my ass…literally.

The next day, Christmas Eve, my punishment was cleaning up after that party. The emptying of those glasses—good heavens, the smell! I vowed never to drink again. That declaration to self did not last long. That day, I finished up and went to work at Dad's store for a few hours. When we arrived home, he gave me a gift. This was not like him, as Mom did all the gift buying. This was something I'd had my eye on for a number of weeks. It was a complete album set from the band Chicago. Some of you may remember the beige cover. There were four records altogether. I knew when Dad presented them to me it was he, this time, who felt shame for his behaviour. This was a first! I was sixteen and Dad was saying once again that he was sorry—not in tears, as he usually did, but in gifts. *Hmm... this feels good.*

The freedom of wheels

That sixteenth summer I received a piece of freedom that came in the form of a motorbike. I was the only girl in Stephenville with a Honda cycle. My friend Karen and I were always on the fly. There is something freeing about the sun in your face, the wind in your hair, and changing gears.

This freedom was short lived; the gears were about to shift.

We did, however, get summer jobs. In the early seventies there was Opportunities for Youth. OFY. They paid us fifty dollars a week for jobs that kept us busy all summer and out of mischief. We applied for the job of lifeguards at the summer recreation center. Problem was I could not swim. Karen could, so with that little piece of freedom we drove to our work daily. We watched the wee ones, cleaned the pool, and no one was the wiser that little Miss Lilly was not a swimmer. We frolicked and played and on weekends when my parents were camping, Karen and I went to the clubs. One in particular was a place called Wheelers.

The fairy meets her knight

It was now September 2, 1973. I was seventeen years old. I drove into the arms of a Mountie.

I arrived, on my motorbike, at a nightclub. Imagine, seventeen-years-young and able to enter a nightclub?

His front tooth was chipped,
he was shy as could be,
but he wanted me
and I wanted he.

It wasn't long a romance did bloom.
It was just us—for other people, no room.
Awkward at first, for we were quite young,
The next thing I knew, "Here Comes The Bride" was being sung.

With hardly a breath and so very fast,
Melanie was born early—she was here, at last, at last.

John was a very shy man. I asked him to dance and wow, he could dance, I was smitten. The hell with the fact his tooth was chipped and he did not know how to dress.

The next evening, Sunday, I took my sister Kathy to see the movie, "Sound of Music." As we were leaving the parking lot, I saw John outside with his grey Vega car looking at the tire. We stopped and offered him a drive. I took him home to meet mom and dad and he could make the phone call to someone about his tires. (No cell phones back then, 1973.)

I found out later that he pretended to have a flat as he had called my home and was told I was at the movies. Sly fox.

He visited for an hour or two, told my parents he was in the RCMPolice, which seemed to impress my father until John opened his mouth and let his jester out. You see John is very shy, (I now know it is Asperger's) and he uses his jester to feel comfortable. On his first meeting with dad, John decided to tell funny jokes about Newfoundland. Now I don't know if you know but if you are from NFLD you can tell funny jokes about yourselves but someone from Nova Scotia, NO, not going to be so funny. (John is from Halifax). After John left my father was like a whore in a fit. He tells me to never bring that so and so home again.

Our Mom is in the kitchen ironing. There were no legs on that iron board and Mom would put it between the stove and counter. I swear that was a form of mediation for mom, ironing, she loved it. As I go to my room across from where she is in her mediation (ironing) she says. I think he's the one for you. Moms are very intuitive when it comes to love. We begin dating. I paid no attention to Dad's warning and he too was soon smitten.

We married in October 1974, just over a year from the time we met. I was carrying Melanie. Mom and Dad asked us to wait until after baby was born to make sure this is what I wanted. John wanted me and I wanted he. There was no going back or waiting. We rented a small house in Pasadena, NFLD the month before our wedding. John was stationed in Corner Brook and Pasadena is just 20 min away. The night of our wedding we wanted to stay at the house to celebrate. My Dad suggested we take a hotel as John's parents and his Aunt Margie and her husband were staying at our wee home. We said no, they'll be wise enough to leave us alone on our wedding night and they will take a hotel. Our wedding was in Stephenville, Pasadena was two hours away in 1974. Didn't happen, at 2:00am I hear sobbing in the living room. Today, years later I wonder if it was giggles. At the time I was alarmed to hear crying and wondered what Fran, my mother –in-law was crying about. Image the gall, arriving at our wee home at 2:00 in the morning. John got up to see if they were ok. I was still angry with them when I got up early. I wore a beautiful long white & blue night grown and robe my mother had given me for our first night together. I made the mistake of going to the window to look outside and the sunlight shone throughout my tiny body. John came over and said," you can see through your gown and maybe you should not be in the window." John has the knight archetype and always protecting. That first day together I can now see he was concerned about his Mother's wishes. This is a great start to a marriage so I simply said, "They have to facking go". They heard me, this was Sunday, they left on Monday.

Our bliss begins in that wee home and I have 6 weeks of it. In those six weeks, I cooked, read cookbooks, encyclopaedias and was in beautiful silence. John was working late shift and would sleep all day. I loved the stillness, as you have to remember I was the oldest of six with a Dad who loved to bark. There was also stillness in John, strength, a grounding I had not experienced before and I was at peace. In those first six weeks I made more lemon pies that did not turn out and over the fence they would go. There was a small creek over that fence and I wonder how many birds, foxes ate those pies. Imagine, DEATH BY PIE.

One evening in late Nov, water was on the floor. It had run out of me and I had no idea what was happening so I called my Aunt Patsy. Girl, get your coat on.

Nuns & roses

What in the…"Hell-o, Aunt Patsy—I stood up and there is water everywhere."

It was Wednesday evening, November 28, 1974. I had just turned nineteen years of age. John had left an hour before to play hockey in Corner Brook. We were living in the small scenic community of Pasadena, NFLD. If you have not visited, you should—it is worth the trip. Marble Mountain was nearby, and we were just twenty minutes from my grandparents in Deer Lake.

Aunt Patsy and Uncle Ambrose were living just a mile away. We had rented a small house there when we had gotten married, just over a month earlier. My parents wanted us to wait until after the baby was born, but John was posted to Corner Brook and he knew what he wanted and that was me.

This "me" who was standing in the middle of our small living room, was barely recognizable with that tummy and swollen hands and feet. Water was flooding between my legs onto the floor and I had no idea what had just happened. I knew enough to pick up the phone and call my aunt. When I explained, she panicked and said I was about to start labour.

"But that is impossible—this baby is not due until January 1975!"

"Get your coat on child, and I will be right there," she replied with authority.

Off to the races is what it felt like. I had pain, but I had experienced pain before so I just numbed out for a while. I talked to an angel or two, looked up towards the bright starry night sky, and breathed in the crisp November air. I had no concept of what was happening.

Within an hour, nuns were spinning around and above me. I was swearing such oaths—I didn't know that I could pronounce such dandy ones! From that moment to this day, I still swear like a truck driver when I am in pain, either emotionally or physically.

But, back to November 28. Near midnight, John finally arrived at the Corner Brook Hospital. That look of a deer in a headlight came over him as he heard me swearing and a nun say, "What language from a youngster! Imagine a child having a child. This is what happens when they play around. Foolish, foolish youngsters."

At one point, as they were talking to each other, I was in another rapture, and I told them to shut the fudge up. They were silenced.

You and I know the word used was not actually "fudge."

Finally, and after much fussing around between the doctors and nuns, I was told that they needed to operate. Even though I was only seven months along, I was too small to deliver. They had to do a Caesarean section.

As I was wheeled down the corridor, John was beside me and I was saying goodbye and telling him I was sorry and that I loved him. You see, in my young mind, I had no idea what a Caesarean section meant. No one bothered, or maybe there was no time, to explain what was about to happen. I was sure that I would have to die for the baby to be born. For some unknown reason (maybe it was youth or the labour pain), I did not feel fear. That is simply what I thought Caesarean meant. The nuns were praying, John was stunned, and I was going to sleep—*Yippee, finally.*

A deep, deep sleep.

I did not awake until eight p.m. the next evening. The curtains were drawn and it was dark inside the room, but God I could smell roses. I will remember that deep fragrance forever. Before I opened my heavy eyelids, I asked, "Angels, is this Heaven?" The smell was intoxicating.

Then I heard, "She is waking up."

Nuns. Those damned nuns were at me again. Angels, what are you doing with me? This is NOT Heaven.

Melanie was born at 1:20 a.m.: four pounds, nine ounces. Big for a preemie baby. She was immediately put into an incubator because her lungs had not yet developed. It was days before I was able to get up and go see her. How abandoned she would have felt. Those first few moments of being, of birthing into a new life are so important, and it's even more important to be touched and nourished by your mother. Melanie did not receive this. Those hours and those days of being alone lived with her for the duration of her short life. So begins another chapter in John's and my life that haunts us to this day.

Melanie was unable to come home until she was two months old. The first week we were able to bring her home, I stayed with my parents. I had just been diagnosed with stomach ulcers and was not feeling well. John was working night shifts with the RCMP and thought I needed care. I am grateful for that decision. The third night, when I was feeding Melanie her bottle, she turned blue. She lay dying in my arms. My father called an ambulance and both of us were flown to the hospital in St. John's, NFLD, as the one in Stephenville had no idea what was happening to our baby. She could not breathe on her own. Once in St. John's, it was discovered she had pyloric stenosis. (Pyloric stenosis is a narrowing of the opening from the stomach to the first part of the small intestine, due to enlargement of the muscle surrounding this opening, which spasms when the stomach empties. This condition causes severe, projectile, non-bilious vomiting and most often occurs in the first few months of life.)

Pyloric stenosis typically develops in male babies aged two to six weeks. As Melanie was a girl and two months old, it was difficult to diagnose.

Once again she was alone. I was able to be with her after surgery, but for a limited time. The bonding that is required for healthy babies was rare for us, and Melanie grew into a withdrawn, angry little girl. I did my best to connect with her, but she continued to push.

I could see at an early age we were in for a battle. She was two; I was twenty-one. There was something about her that made her seem older than me. There were days I wanted to cuddle, but she would have none of it. At that time, she was a loner in her crib or her room, with a look of sadness deep in her eyes. As a mother I felt a failure. It took me years to understand how important the first few hours and months are to a baby and his or her development.

We are transferred to Fredericton, NB, in 1975

We brought our baby home for six months and were transferred to Fredericton, NB. I was overjoyed—I was leaving Newfoundland. I was to young to understand the beauty this island held and the history, the labour of the people, and the dignity of the islanders.

We were in Fredericton and it felt like paradise. We purchased our first home with a down payment from a hardtop trailer that Dad had given us as a wedding gift. We had not had time to use it, and the deposit on our home on Hartt Street was a gift we could not have afforded if not for Dad.

John was busy working in with the Royal Canadian Mounted Police, and we became fast friends with Bob and Loretta. Bob was John's boss. He and Loretta reminded me of my parents, but without the rules.

Our neighbours were young like ourselves; Elaine and Ralph, Rose and Randy, Corrine and Hazen. They had small children also, and we acquired tools of living from each other.

Life seemed easy except for throwing John's clothes over the railing a few days a month, when he was away playing too much hockey. I said to him one day: "It's me or your hockey."

Without a breath, his reply: "I've known my hockey longer than I've known you."

You can only imagine where his clothes ended up that day. It took him a few days before he was allowed into the house.

All was forgiven, we were juvenile.

The drunken labour

It was not long before I was pregnant again. I was sick from the moment of conception to Amanda's birth. At the time, no one really knew why we could vomit twenty-four hours a day for nine months. Now they call it Hyperemesis Gravidarum, (severe nausea and vomiting during pregnancy). I was in and out of hospital for IV so I would not become dehydrated.

The baby was not due until late December, but I went into labour early once again.

Finally, in my seventh month, I was admitted to the new hospital they had just built in Fredericton: Dr. Everett Chalmers Regional. I was tucked away into a private room and they put on a drip to stop the sickness and contractions.

At exactly 1:05 a.m., the nurses decided it was time to call John. I was up out of bed and had pulled the drip from my arm. I was singing, being rowdy and wild, waking other patients, and would not stop laughing, dancing, and swearing. It looked like I was inebriated, drunk, sloshed. Yes, at that time in 1976, they had given me an alcoholic drip to stop the contractions. The look on John's face when he came into the room was both stunned and horrified. He did not know what to do with me. I remember, even in my intoxicated state, seeing his deer-in-the-headlights stare again. I do not think he had ever seen me this way. (That was to come a few years later).

Finally, between him and the nurses, they decided to call my doctor. By six am, I was carried away by an ambulance into Saint John, NB. Because Dr. Everett Chalmers Regional Hospital was new, they did not have a prenatal unit. I remember John driving our old 1967 Chevy at high speeds to be in Saint John before us, and he was.

I stayed in the hospital for two months: October 1 to December 1, 1976.

I stayed in that bed from October 1 to November 15. Yes, I was not allowed to move for fear of going into early labour again. They brought me my bedpan, washed my body and my hair, all in bed. I witnessed so many new mothers-to-be come, stay, and leave my room for those two months.

That was the first time Melanie was in Newfoundland with my parents and siblings for an extended time. Six months later, she was to return, when John discovered he had cancer.

I was sent home December 1, 1976. I remember being so happy to be home-based. Melanie would not arrive in New Brunswick until after this baby's birth.

On December 6, my grandfather, James Smith, passed away while living with my parents. I received the call the first thing on Monday morning. The next day, I was again in labour and a Caesarean section was preformed at 6:35 a.m. on Wednesday morning. While I was in recovery, my grandfather was standing at the edge of my bed. He told me we had another girl. I recall him so vividly. He said his goodbye and told me we would be fine, and that it was time for him to leave.

When I was wheeled out and saw John, I said, "Granddad just told me we have another daughter." John thought I was still on the drugs from operation and chuckled.

The doctor told us that when he went in to remove the baby, he took my appendix and tied my tubes; I could not have any more babies. Three was a dream, but two was enough.

In all the years between then and now, I have been satisfied that we were to only have two children. A boy was not to be, but that was just fine with me.

Melanie arrived home the following week and, as my mother walked the tiny girl in her beautiful pink corduroy snowsuit, up the back steps, I tried to pick my daughter up. She would have none of me. It must have been very confusing for her, away from us. Two months can be a lifetime to a two-year-old.

I knew and I felt that Melanie and I were in for conflict. She did not allow me to touch her. Not allowing me to touch her ends up lasting a lifetime. This is the beginning of her anger; my belief is that this is the beginning of her madness—her addictions, which are to raise their ugly heads in her twelfth year. Of course I was not aware of any of this at the time. All I knew was that I was being rejected. She did however form a bond with her father and for this I was grateful.

The twin

We were going up in the elevator. "You have to be kidding me. God, this is not funny anymore." Jim, John's twin, was in front of me. It was 1977. Melanie was two, Amanda was just six months, and the doctors were telling me that John, my husband of two years, was going to die.

Jim and I were returning from visiting John, and I told Jim, "If anything happens to John, I cannot see you again; you look too much alike. How will I ever cope or get over him?! Please, do not take this personally, but fudge, life is nuts, there are two of you!"

It was all very strange. Was I crazy? *Dr. Death, go away. You cannot have him. John is dying, but not on my watch.* I was twenty-one, he was twenty-five…

That watch has lasted for forty-one years. John is still with us, and healthier than he has ever been.

We had settled into a routine for a few months after Amanda's birth, until one day in March 1977, John came home and said, "I think I have cancer." He was in the kitchen at the time, leaning up against the counter, looking forlorn, and I told him he was nuts. "Actually," he said, "it's funny you use that word…One of my testicles is very swollen. It has been for a few months."

His stepfather had just been diagnosed with cancer a year before, so I thought John was just panicking.

In May, he was in hospital having his right testicle removed, and indeed his doctor told him it was malignant. They called me into John's room and told us both that it had spread into his lymph nodes and more surgery was required. This time the operation would be in Halifax, Nova Scotia.

Is our life just beginning or ending?

At least we were able to relieve a bit of the doctor's sorrow. He felt terrible about the diagnosis but also about the fact that we could not have any more children. I, in my nervousness, began to laugh out loud and explained to him that he was off the hook on that one. I'd had my fallopian tubes tied six months earlier. We were blessed to have the two we had and grateful we'd had them early or they would not have existed.

I remember the first night at hospital with John, once we were told. They put a bed in his room for me and he kept saying, "When I die, you have to promise me you'll die with me." I was so confused, as I knew he was scared, but I also knew we had two children to raise. It made me furious that he would ask that question, yet my heart ached. I was frantic because I did not want to be left behind, and I was aching because I did not want him to leave me.

We flew into Halifax and my parents took Melanie back to Newfoundland while I was with John during surgery. They removed most of his lymph nodes and told us he was fortunate they'd found everything when they did or he would have ended up with lung cancer as well. (To someone who never smoked, this was a shock.)

He was discharged a month later, Melanie was returned home to us, and we picked up the pieces and started over.

Melanie became more withdrawn than ever, and I was in no mood to try to humour her. I had a sick husband, a baby less than a year old, and I was starting to reorganize my life. Poor little two-year-old—she did not really have a chance at a normal life.

My drinking days were beginning. I had drunk when I was a teenager but stopped once married and having the children. The day we found out John's cancer was malignant, I clearly remember asking a friend who was at our home, "Pour me a drink?" For the next few years, that was my mantra: Poor me, poor me, pour me a drink.

John took his chemo every three weeks while I was working at the Bank of Nova Scotia. There was a shadow over our home—something I cannot explain. It was heavy, hopeless. John took his medicine; I took my medication—booze.

The fairy falls off her pedestal

It was a Sunday morning and John had had many doses of chemo. He usually vomited from morning to night. His treatments were every three weeks for two years. (A lifetime when you are twenty-two and twenty-five.)

That morning he said he was hungry, so I got up to make him his favourite; poached eggs. Once they were ready, I went to get him, but he was still in the washroom. I knocked on the door and slowly entered. He was sitting on the edge of the bathtub, most of his thick auburn hair in the wastebasket.

Reality set in. This was real.

Next day, I went to see his doctor with our seven-month-old on my lap. "Doctor," I asked, "what is this disease and what can I expect?"

"What do you do?" was his reply.

"I am a homemaker with two small children. Why?"

"Well," he said, "in less than five years, you will probably be a widow. Go get yourself a job."

Now it was my time to vomit. I quickly went home and downed a dark rum and coke. It was the first time that I remember having a drink to release the pain or distress. I had a drink to play or to take risks, but never to release pain before.

Pain was now the next baggage that I packed to put on this train. If I was going to be a widow at twenty-five, I'd better get educated.

I am not sure if I was in madness or in my addiction. At the time I didn't even think of such things. I was in survival mode.

I started taking a business course at UNB, the university in Fredericton. It was a few night courses. I never finished them. I was busy with kids. I did, however, learn enough about bookkeeping to get myself a job at

Superior Acceptance, Woolco's credit department. My boss, Joyce, was a wonderful woman. She taught me all I needed to know, but within six months we were told that Woolco was taking the credit department to Toronto. They were closing down the office. But after six months of my working for her, Joyce had so much faith in me that she literally took me to the Bank of Nova Scotia and said, "Hire this girl."

They hired me as a clerk-typist. Thing is, I couldn't type! Whether it was Joyce's promoting me, or my enthusiasm, or my looks, (I am not sure which came first), but I worked that job part-time for three years from 9:00 a.m. to 1:00 p.m. The archetype of Miss Congeniality took over—I loved that job! I would take people through the interview process for loan applications. What letters I couldn't type, I paid off the typists upstairs to type for me. Those typing pool girls became my best friends. It wasn't long before I was repaying my debt to them with drinks at a bar. Friday nights couldn't come fast enough.

Slowly, you could feel the addictions seeping in. The pain of running a household at such a young age, looking after two children, going deeper into debt with daycare and John's chemo treatments, were all reasons for me (as wrong as they were) to find an outlet.

All was grand and I entered into a deeper level of madness.

I took the children out to a babysitter.

I make no excuses for such bad behaviour, but oh my God those times, they were so funny. The dichotomy of the light and shadow started to raise its ugly head.

One night in particular comes to my memory. After a night at a club, I went to my vehicle; it was our '67 Chevy. The parking lot was up three floors. No problem—I got into my car, settled in, listened to the sounds of the night, the buzzing—*No wait, I think that is my head.* Oh well, homeward bound. Suddenly I heard a click, scrape, bang. I didn't see anything, so I headed down the ramp. Home to faithful John and Hartt Street.

I got out of the car and had made my way around it to climb the stairs to our back door, when something caught my eye. It was what was NOT seen that I saw. The passenger door was missing. *What the hell?!* Actually, it was, "What the fuck?!" I had a mouth like a truck driver in those days, so swearing came naturally to me. I began to chuckle, but then

47

the seriousness of what had happened hit me. I would have to go in and tell John that the sound I had heard while driving down the ramp was the missing door. I must not have closed it, probably after I climbed into the car through the passenger side, as I had parked too close to the wall. *Oh shite, I'm in trouble now—again.* I entered the house very quietly, hoping John would be asleep, so at least I could get a good night's sleep and sober up before I told him about my calamity.

As I entered the kitchen, it was not John who met me, but our neighbour Paul. It appeared that John was out and about looking for me. Hmm, this had never happened before. Paul said John figured I was with the gang from the bank and at the club, and that is where he went. *Oh boy—trouble times two. Now what do I do?! I can't lie my way out of this.*

Within minutes, John was home. Paul bid us adieu and silently left before the shit hit the fan.

As I saw the look on John's face, I was not chuckling any more. All he said to me was, "I always had you on a pedestal."

I had fallen. John was not one to ever say he loved me or show his affection, so I was shocked. But not as shocked as he was when I showed him the car. No words were spoken for a few weeks. We went about our lives in silence. This became a pattern, this silence. It was years later that I realized I was an addict, and John had a level of Asperger's Syndrome (delays in the development of many basic skills; most notably the ability to socialize with others, to communicate, and to use imagination). That was why he was unable to express himself. He was unable to say mine or the girls' names aloud. He never looked at us (or anyone) directly in the eye, or thought positively about most aspects of life. (Saying all this about him, please remember he was loyal, strong, and faithful; the knight to this fairy queen.)

Our daughters didn't have a hope in hell. Or did they?

1979: Crazy Nellie. Silly Lilly.

Have you ever known something, but everyone around you is saying that you are crazy or silly? Have you experienced severe pain and suffering, which you know is real, yet you cave in and buy what others are telling you? (Prostitute in my shadow) Selling out.

It happened innocently enough. I was twenty-four and working at Scotiabank. One morning before I went to work, the girls were at a sitter's, and I decided to try yoga. It was not as well known in the late seventies, but I was excited about learning something new. Halfway through the session, my back went out and I could not move. Seriously—they had to bring me to the hospital. Because of the pain, they decided to keep me in. I contacted John's mother, Fran, in Halifax, and she willingly flew into Fredericton to look after the girls. John was working shift work at this time due to his chemo treatments.

I spent three or four days going through test after test, but they could not find anything. On a rainy Thursday afternoon, the doctor came into my room, sat down, took my hand, and said, "Mrs. White, we cannot find anything wrong in your body and believe the pain is in your head. We believe, my colleagues and I, that due to the fact that you have two children under the age of five, a job, and a husband who is ill, you are experiencing a nervous breakdown."

Well, I was never a nervous person and was not sure what he was talking about. I was only twenty-four.

He suggested I transfer up to the second floor, to the psychiatric ward. *Oh what the hell—I need the rest.* Up I went and sat on the bed as the nurse registered me. Luckily for me, I knew the nurse, Patsy. Her husband was in the RCMP. She was very mothering and not judgmental. She began asking questions. "No, I really am not worried about anything. John is going to live, if I have to kill him to do it. The girls are fine, I like my job, I owe $500 on my Visa—not sure why I am having a breakdown… whatever that is."

Jesus, Mary, and all that is holy, just as she was finishing up with me, in walked my roommate. She was between sixty-five and seventy—hard to say—her hair was long and grey, she was skinny and in her nightdress. She walked into the middle of the room, pulled up her nightdress, and urinated on the floor.

Okay, this is weird. Is this what a breakdown looks like? Hmm, I hadn't had a desire to do that. Patsy the nurse left, and I crawled into the bed on my back that was not hurting, although I was in agony every time I moved my legs. I pulled the covers over myself and started to cry. *How did this happen? Where the hell am I, really?*

My roommate's name was Nellie; the underwear less shadow of a woman. That night, as we both lay awake, I asked her questions. I wanted to know her story. As I write this, I want to cry, thinking about Nellie. She had never married. Her fiancé had been killed in the war, and she never got over him. When Nellie was in bed, maybe because of a drug they gave her, she would talk for hours and was very intelligent. Come morning, it was like someone else had entered her body. She was smelly, mumbling to herself, and pissing all over the place. I am not making this up.

Saturday, I went into a room with a psychiatrist, and he gave me a shot of something. It was supposed to be a truth serum.

I started talking. All I could talk about was Nellie and the book I was reading, *The Thorn Birds*. He continued to ask me questions, and I remember him feeling me up, asking if I felt anything. "Yes," I said, "your hands all over my privates, and I am married." We discussed my marriage, and the only thing he could get out of me was that I was afraid that John might die and…"Hands off me, please. I don't know you that well yet."

End of session.

Sunday—a normal day with Nellie. Monday, I called my friend, Rose Ford. "Come get me the hell out of here!" (I am not sure where John was—he must have been working.)

I went to the front desk to discharge myself, and I told them *they* were nuts—not me. My back still hurt, and I did not need to smell any more piss and be felt up by a lunatic. They politely told me that the doctor had not discharged me. I told them to go pound sand—I was outta there. They said they were not responsible for me if I left—that I had to sign a document. I told them, "NO, you certainly are NOT responsible for me. Give me that document and you know what you can do with it after."

Poor Rose—I am sure at this point she thought I was nuts.

When we got in her car, I asked her to make a detour to Woolco. I had my family allowance on me—a twenty-six dollar cheque. I proceeded to purchase underwear, pantyhose, and a nightdress and brought them back to Nellie. After just an hour or so of being apart, when I returned to give the items to Nellie, she did not remember me. Oh well, I did what spirit had instructed me to do.

I was finished with Nellie. Or so I thought.

Six months later I was working at my desk at Scotiabank (The Bank of Nova Scotia in the seventies) when my phone rang. I was working in ledgers and I heard a familiar voice say, "Hello, this is Nellie McCloud." (Not her real name.) "Can you check my account balance for me? I need someone from the bank to bring me a cheque so I can pay my mortgage."

"Yes, Nellie," I replied. "Please hold." I was in shock to know she could even phone the bank, and stunned to find out her balance was over a million dollars, plus she had war bonds. OK, maybe all that money drove her over the edge. Who knows? You know that saying: "Never judge a book by its cover?" Never judge a woman from her smell or nightdress. I had purchased her underwear, as I thought she did not have a pot to pee in, she liked doing it on the floor so much. Maybe every time she piddled, she was harvesting her pot of gold.

In between those six months, I did find out why I was in pain. A friend of mine, Corinne C., suggested I see her chiropractor. When he took x-rays, he showed me that I had mini- scoliosis: a deep curve in the spine and a deteriorating disk. If it was not looked after, there was a possibility that I would be in a wheelchair by the time I was fifty. He explained that the reason the doctors did not see it was that they take x-rays while the patient is lying down; with the chiropractor, I was standing up.

(My brother Derek had severe scoliosis. Our mom had TB when she carried us, and I am convinced that is the root cause.)

I saw this chiropractor for a few months, until he began to fondle me and ask me out. He knew I was as married he was. I did not return. For some reason, when I saw him at a dance that John and I were at that Christmas, I felt shame. Had I led him on? No, I had not. He did not interest me. Why should I feel the shame? Old habits are hard to break.

The sigh

"That is a sign of a restless soul."

I was very young at the time, and the word "soul" was something I wanted to know more about. She explained that I was lost; I was looking for something that I already had. Well, you can imagine, she had my attention. That well had been empty for many years, though I found various ways to fill it; sugar, drink, and spending, to name a few. It is interesting to me that "well," a hole in the ground, is the same word for being healthy.

Have you ever noticed how many times a day you, or those around you, sigh? How deep is your sigh? Are you complaining, yearning, and moaning? Or are you merely tired and needing to catch your breath?

Sighing can become an addiction. I have watched many who live in their Victim and do not know there is a way out of the well. If it does not drive them mad, it certainly drives those around them into being annoyed. In my life there was such an individual. I loved her dearly and she passed in 2005. I never knew anyone who sighed so often. She was an example of the Goddess of Beauty. Everything about her was elegant and chic. She could have been a magazine model. However, she was the model of the walking wounded: her mannerisms, her speech, her tone, her distress, her sighs.

An abundance of debt

All my life I have had weighty concerns about finances. I've had too much or not enough.

My first memory of money is taking twenty dollars from my father's cash box, which he kept under his bed. I was nine. Dad had a sporting goods store in Stephenville: Hancock's Sport Shop. At the time, it looked like we had it all. We were living on credit and the bank, but hey, we had a business, so other people's perception was what Dad led them to believe. That twenty dollars I took, for who knows what reason, was a large amount at the time. I remember going to McClellan's store and buying candy. I bought so much that I could not keep it all, so I gave it all away. Easy come—easy go. This is a tough chapter. Not because I do not want to talk about it, but because it has so many threads.

"DEBT. YOU WILL ALWAYS HAVE FINANCIAL DEBT IF YOU ARE IN ENERGETIC DEBT." I first heard these words from Shankari, a very wise woman, whom I met when I was studying with Doreen Virtue. I was on my second visit to Bali. Shankari was finishing her book, and I had the privilege of being with her as she read those words. I have never forgotten them.

In 1977, John was on chemo and we were raising two beautiful beings of light. Usually when we purchased groceries we were together, but this Friday evening he had his chemo treatment so I was alone. I returned home with a $71 food receipt. A High bill for 1977.

He was shocked. He sat down on the dining room chair and said, "There is a mistake. This bill is so high; they made an error."

I watched him add up every item bent over with his bald head (from the treatments). No, there was no mistake. I was in trouble. How could

I explain the amount and not have him worry? I made a deal with the shadow theif: never again would I tell him the truth about what things cost.

I was working at the Bank of Nova Scotia at the time. There were babysitting, gas, and food expenses. I started slashing expenses in half. If babysitting was $60 a month for two children, I told him it was $30. If the food was $100 for two weeks, I told him it was $50. I did not want to worry him. He had enough on his plate; he was trying to survive. How did I hide it? I had the gold from Never, Neverland… the almighty Charge It. That is what Visa was called in those days. Jesus, I had a rainbow, right there in my pocket.

By the year 1979, I was in immense debt without John knowing. I was not spending on clothes, as my mother still had her dress shop and was sending me clothes monthly. She closed the store later that year. My debt was from everyday living; babysitters, groceries, and the clubs.

To kill or not to kill

Those were days of light and shadow. One such day, John awoke with the announcement that he wouldn't take any more chemo treatments. Now you must remember, he was into his second year, taking these treatments every three weeks. He used to get sick driving to the hospital on Friday, just thinking about them. And it would be Monday before he would arise again. So when he rose this one day saying that he wouldn't take any more treatments, I understood. However, that did not mean I agreed. As he continued to repeat, "No more," saying he would rather die, I decided to kill him. It wasn't a conscious decision; just my Archetype Queen's reaction to his self-pity. (Archetypes are energy of behaviours, patterns that live in each of us and in the collective) My anger flared and I picked up a radio he had given me when I was eighteen years old. It was in the shape of a knight and heavy! I picked it up and threw it at him. If he hadn't ducked, it would have hit him right between the eyes. It left a hole in the wall that stayed there until we sold the house in 1982, three years later.

He got up and went for his treatment. I guess he figured it was better to die from his treatment than at the hands of a wicked wife. Death was not his destiny. Just before he got his clean bill of health, he was fated to possibly die, but not at my hands.

One such weekend of John's treatment, his white blood count was low so chemo was postponed until the following weekend. He was to work shift work that Friday night with a chap by the name of Lidstone. Another police officer took John's place; his name was Brophy. The phone rang early Saturday morning, and John was told the two officers had been shot to death at a home dispute. John was white, not from his treatment but from shock and guilt. He was alive because he might have died if he did not take his chemo. What a dreadful irony.

We and the RCMP families of New Brunswick went into deep mourning. If John hadn't been thinking he was going to live his life well, he now pulled his own rank on himself and he decided life was worth living.

It was soon after this event that John started to activate his Athlete Archetype. He had always been a hockey and baseball player, but now he became an avid runner, running for his life. John continued his treatments and by the end of 1981, after five years, there were two awards for him: a clean bill of health, and a French immersion course through the RCMP.

In those years we lived in Madness, and I in Addiction. Through it all, there was always a love between us. A bond, bondage, or a bandage?

Our next journey was to begin: a transfer to St. Leonard, NB. As a family, we choose to live in Grand Falls, only twenty minutes away.

In June 1982, we arrive in Grand Falls, NB. We were about to begin a new life in farmland and potato country in New Brunswick…home of McCain's.

The Grand of Grand Falls. Falling into Madness.

Thank God, we were leaving Fredericton—all those memories of John's illness, our crazy orange shag carpet, my drinking and attempts at finding new survival skills.

The first people we were introduced to were the most normal, balanced family I had ever met. I was in awe of the love they had for one another. Everything was "No problem." "It's a great day." They were hardworking, loyal people and were doing projects in other parts of the world to help those less fortunate. They were doing these things long before it became the norm for an average family. There were always people in their home from different parts of the world that needed help. They were idealistic; filled with love, hope, and compassion. And by God they lived it! They did not talk about it—they ate, slept, and hugged it into themselves and their four children.

I felt like I had hit a jackpot in becoming friends with this family. My girls loved them; they had daughters the same age and the kids quickly became friends. Conrad and his brother Claude were potato farmers and the hardest working people I had met to date. Linda, Conrad's wife, and I soon became friends. She was ten years older, but that did not matter. There was a rhythm to our togetherness, a beat that I did not understand at the time, but I certainly do now as I write this. We both are holistic participators. We began studying around the same time many years ago, after we left in 1986 when we were not living in the same town. Neither of us would know what the other was doing, but eventually we discovered we were on the same path in our personal spiritual growth.

There was a rocking chair in the middle of their kitchen, and this became my throne whenever I visited. I would rock, tell a story or two, and listen to their wisdom. I adored this family and continue to love and admire them to this day.

Some of my madness, they were able to experience with us, but not once were we judged. All we ever received from them was love.

It was here in Grand Falls that I realized I had an anger issue. I took it upon myself one day to go see a therapist. I made the decision after I threw every dish from the dinner table into the dishwasher. I was so angry with Melanie over something small that I wanted to take her and shake her. Instead I broke all the dishes. I had a problem so to the doctor I did go.

He asked me many things about my past, but at the ripe old age of twenty-nine I did not think my past was an issue. I was angry *now*. I wanted answers *now*.

I went to see him a few times. We talked plenty about my father, but I still did not see the connection. I told him my dreams about trains; he said that was the father's penis. No, I KNOW I have never been sexually abused. That I know with every fibre of my being. The doctor was getting nowhere with me, so I stopped going. One day in March, I was ironing the girls' clothes; we were leaving to take them to Disney World in Florida the next day.

The phone rang. "Is this Mrs. White?"

"Yes," I replied. "Who is this?"

"This is Dr. Black's office. It seems you have missed your last few appointments."

"Yes," I responded. "I do not think he is helping me."

"I am afraid, Mrs. White, that if you do not keep your appointments we are to tell the authorities that you are a potential child abuser."

Jesus, Mary, and all that is holy. *WHAAAAT?!* "Okay, I will be there when I return from taking our potentially abused children to Disney world."

I hung up stunned and kept ironing. John arrived home. I was too filled with shame to tell him about the call.

We left for Florida, returned, and I went back to see that doctor. He saw me for another two sessions and freed me from entrapment. I was finished with him.

A few months later I was in Alberta visiting my parents to recover from a car accident. My mother was ironing and I was telling her it is not easy raising children. She got angry. "What the hell is wrong with you kids today? Do you think it was easy raising six of you?"

"No Mom, I am sure it was not, but one thing I know to be true is this: if you were raising us today, both you and Dad would be in jail. Dad for his beatings, his abuse; you for allowing it to happen."

She put the iron down and left the kitchen. I was left feeling shame for having told the truth.

I returned home to the Grand of Grand Falls but something was different in me. I did not understand, but I was living my life as best as I could. I was hired by a radio station in Pre Isle, Maine, selling advertising, so I didn't need a work visa. I travelled weekly for our Friday meetings and dinners. Once again, Friday was a drinking night. We were living in a home on River Road known as the Fish Hatchery. We didn't have to pay rent, only look after the house. This space and so much in my life was bittersweet. It was a lovely place, but the purple shag carpet made me nuts. The mice and I didn't like each other much either. We fought regularly. The sweet spot was that there were beautiful falls right behind the house and I went there daily to just be. It was the space that allowed me to find something inside that had been hiding. Once I left the space, I was in the house and either drinking or upset about something or other. It was the year of Pac man, so me being me, I wanted to discover as much about this game as I could. I now realize that when something new was open or available to us, I was number one in line to learn.

Melanie was nine, Amanda, seven. The last summer we were in Grand Falls, Amanda was hospitalized for severe headaches. She was there for a week. We were worried, but there was no diagnosis. The only thing the doctor told us is that she may have had stress issues. She'd been learning French, had a father who was ill, and her mother had just had a serious car accident where the car was totalled. (No, I was not drinking that day.) It was years later when Amanda was an adult that she realized she is celiac.

Once she cut out wheat and dairy from her diet, her headaches stopped, and she had a wee bit of weight gain, finally. She was always so thin. We can now breathe, but at this earlier point in time I was not connecting the dots between what we ate and the madness we felt. That was to come later.

We were in this small town of Grand Falls, which housed nearly 6000 people, for four years. I made many friends and caused much damage. Some of these friends love me today and I am in deep gratitude , true friends are our soul companions.

In August 1986, we were transferred to one of my favourite places: Bouctouche, NB. It is a small community on the water, about forty minutes from Moncton. It is where JC Irving was born.

The transfer was a relief for me, as I needed to run again. People were about to find me out.

The Madness of ME

In 1987 we were living in Bouctouche, NB. The girls were twelve and ten. I considered myself old at the time; thirty-two. I thought I had lost my youth. Now that I write this, I realize I had grown up quickly. Sure I was young, but overall I was mature for my age. Most of my close friends at the time, except for Nicole, were ten years older than me.

This one morning, I noticed my Mary Kay had been used and I was confused. I went into the kitchen to prepare breakfast for the chicklets, and I noticed that Melanie's face was made up. Hmm, the answer to the mystery of Mary Kay disarray.

At first I was angry (because she didn't ask), then became enchanted. Even at the young age of thirty-two, before I began any spiritual journey into awareness, I knew this to be a truth: "You have a mere seventeen seconds to grab people's attention. The rest of the time they are thinking of themselves." (I learnt this from my sales background.)

Now, bear with me, this was the late eighties. Today we have become more evolved consciously (at least I hope we have), and we have learnt to focus on one another.

I asked Melanie, "Do you think that you have put all that on your face to ask for attention?"

She gulped down her porridge and said, "Don't know."

I chuckled as Amanda and I rolled our eyes. I tried to explain that how she looked did not matter; she was beautiful and looked like her dad. (And she loved him like no other.) What mattered was being herself, being kind, and being honest. If she could outrun seventeen seconds then great, go for it, but I promised her no one cared, for they were worried about what SHE thought of them. That ever-evolving mirror, the Madness of Me.

The Madness of Me in our culture was, and still is, like a fungus; growing slowly, and somehow becoming our reality. Think of what is spent daily on beauty products, when we could be putting that money towards educating our children about working on the inside; their self-esteem, meditation practices, their compassion. Having said this, however, I believe there is hope for our grandchildren, as both the times and the educating of these children are changing.

If we are always worried about what we look like on the outside, and not how we feel on the inside, we begin to suffer from soul sickness. In Melanie's life, not bonding with her mother, being transferred to different schools in so short a time, possibly left her with a soul sickness. It was easier for her to witness herself only through what others thought of her. Much like I did. She went off to school anyway, wearing her own kind of mask. As she matured, she was much like her mother; she had many masks and wore them deceptively. The apple does not fall far from the tree.

Brushes with Spirit in Rexton

John worked at the Bouctouche detachment for three years. We lived there for two years and purchased a home just twenty minutes away in the wee town of Rexton. Melanie went to a regular school and Amanda to French school, as her language aptitude was high. Melanie joined Cadets here and was very happy. I was working for a magazine—*The Atlantic Advocate*—and travelled back and forth to Fredericton. I also sold clothing at night in friends' homes from a Montreal-based company called La Relance. Everything in this small town was moving along in a normal fashion. We looked like the perfect family. I was drinking still, but mostly when I was on the road. I had a few friends in Rexton who drank with me, but only on rare occasions. We were in Rexton for a year and I have two vivid memories. These memories hold lessons.

The first one was the day Melanie walked down the stairs from her bedroom in her Cadet uniform. I nearly fainted. At the time, I was not much into past lives, but the night before I'd had a dream of being in the Second World War as a Jew, and a man was looking for me. I hid behind a table, but he found me and pulled his gun. I awoke when the bullet hit my head. When I saw Mel, I felt she was the man in my dream. It felt eerie and disturbing to me, especially with the state of continued testing that was our relationship, although she was only thirteen. I did not say anything about the dream, but I did not want her to join the Cadet program. She would have none of my reasons and joined anyway. It would later turn out it was a good decision for her—actually, it was bittersweet—but more about this later.

The second memory is one about humility. One Saturday evening, just before going to sleep, I asked John a question: "John, if there is one thing you would change about me, what would it be?"

He didn't take time to think about it, but answered, "Humility." I had no idea what the word meant. I awoke the next morning and opened the Bible he had given me a few years previously. The Catholic book of worship. It immediately opened to Sirach 10:6 to 10:30. The parts that spoke to me were:

10:15 The roots of the proud God plucks up to plant the humble in their place.

10:27 My son, with humility, have self-esteem; prize yourself as you deserve.

I was stunned. I knew Spirit was around me as the room was chilled. I was frightened also, as I'd had many experiences of feeling Spirit around me but never speaking to me in this way. I closed the book and prayed.

For a few days I kept going back to that section in the Bible and reread it until I remembered the message by heart. *Okay, I will learn what humility means.* Another journey was about to begin.

I was finding out that Madness and Addiction are one.

We are all given a wee bit of Madness. Use it wisely

It was 1989 and we were living in Port Elgin, NB. Our oldest daughter, Melanie, was fourteen. She was beautiful, independent. There was always a consequence to our saying, "No," to her. I was JUST beginning to understand that.

It was October, and she was going to a Halloween dance, or so she thought. We had three rules in our home: bring your laundry to the washer, no long-distance phone calls, and no lying. She had not been able to comply with any of them.

She was walking down the stairs. We were living in the RCMP barracks at the time, so our voices were low. "Where are you going, Mel?"

"Out with my friends," her reply.

"I do not think so. Remember we gave you a week to follow simple rules of the White house and you were not able to comply, so I am sorry, no dance."

The shit hit the fan, in all directions. It was so toxic that, for the first time in her fourteen venerable years and me in my late thirties, I caved in. "Okay. Go."

Ah, the knight in the house, the one who kept a witness to the two queens in his castle, finally stepped in and said, "NO, you are NOT going to any dance. You did not do as your mother has requested, therefore you will go back to your room."

There was DEAD silence.

I was shocked; she was numb and stunned. She went to her room in tears.

All was well, or so I believed.

I was working for the *Atlantic Advocate* at the time, a magazine owned by the Irving group. I was one of the first women in the eighties to have a management position there. We had moved to Port Elgin, a three-hour drive away, but I did not want to give up the job I loved, so I travelled back and forth.

So the next day I left for Fredericton and work. I was away for two days. Upon returning home to Port Elgin and entering the front door, John met me. "We need to talk," he said. "Let's go for a drive."

Hmm...something's up—this is not like him.

It appears that Mel was so upset that her dad had said "No" to her for the first time that she reported me to her guidance counsellor, saying I had abused her. Now, try to understand if you can: he is a cop in charge, he has been promoted, and at this point in his career his wife is being investigated for child abuse.

I loved my daughter, but in this moment, in this long dive into hell, I hated her. If I could have shaken her, I would have shaken her awake. Are you in your Madness, Melanie? Neither your father nor I have never ever laid a hand on you. That you would manipulate your beliefs this way is unforgiveable. I shake you many a times and verbally abuse you. Not because I am in control, but because I had no control.

Oh darling girl, what have you done? Now more healing has just begun.

We love our children and we try to feel their pain; so when Melanie arrived home that evening, all was forgiven. I was investigated, nothing was found, and life as we knew it in this hellish town of 300 souls was back to normal. Normal for me was my date with Captain Morgan. I drank at least once a day between five and six p.m. while making dinner. Sometimes I had more, and I began to notice changes in my mood swings. Most times I felt a sense of peace, other days not so much.

During this time, John was applying for another promotion; another transfer to another town. It would be a promotion to officer status. In the RCMP, you begin your career as a constable, and then if you are promoted, become a sergeant, next, a staff sergeant, and then an officer. John explained that if he got this promotion, it would be beneficial to our retirement. I was not so sure at the time, for the moving had had its consequences on our children. The Madness of chasing the carrot. The Addiction to power.

Feb 1991: John arrives home weighed down

He passed the exam but not the interview. "What the fudge?!!!" I replied. *Holy hell, we are going to be stuck here in a town of 326 souls, living their lives in boredom with nowhere to go. Hmm, this is not for me.*

It was a Tuesday afternoon; two p.m. To heck with it, I was having a drink. I could not believe the destiny we were heading for. Our fate was sealed, or was it?! My brain was alive. That first drink was yummy and hot in my tummy. I was brave. I picked up the phone and called John's boss.

"Hello, is Staff Sergeant so-and-so available?"

"No, he is not," was the reply.

"Could you please give me his boss's phone number?"

"Yes, hold on please."

A minute passed; I was still feeling heat in my belly and fire in my brain. I was not staying there in Port Elgin, NB.

I received the number for an officer in Moncton and I repeated the question: "Is Officer so-and-so available? This is Sergeant John White's wife."

"No," was the reply.

"Can you please transfer me to his boss?"

"Yes, one moment please."

I was transferred to a superintendent in Fredericton; a lovely man John and I had met many times through John's hockey. He'd always treated us with the upmost respect.

"Hello, Mrs. White. What can I do for you today?"

"Well, Chief Superintendent, I want to know if there is life after no?" (The "no" to John's application to be an officer.)

"Mrs. White, did you prepare for a no?"

"What?" I replied. "Are you kidding me? Do you think I would have dragged our two daughters to this hellhole? Do you think I would leave the *Atlantic Advocate*, the job of my dreams, and our beautiful home we were living in for only nine months?" (After the Melanie incident, I had resigned from my work.) "No sir, I and the we in thee, did not prepare for a no."

He told me he was sorry but regulations were policy, and for now I must accept my fate.

"No," I replied. "When you transfer an employee of yours, you transfer the whole family. We have an opinion and if we did not have one in the past, we sure as hell do now. I do not mean to be disrespectful sir, but this is not my fate. I am alive and will choose my own destiny. It's not living in this dump, in Port Elgin. I too have a life and will continue with a career!"

We hung up.

I had another drink.

It took two days. Then John walked through the back door. Remember, we were living in barracks, so his voice was low. "Did you call someone recently at head office?"

Oops. "Yes," is my reply. "Why?"

"Well, it seems we both have an interview with someone from head office tomorrow."

"Good," I said. I was not sure if John was angry or in awe. He was a man of few words at this time in our lives. His world revolved around his work and we didn't talk much.

The next day we met a man, who in a few years would be John's boss with the UN in East Timor. He was stern, trying to intimidate me, but I'd been up against men like him before: my father, the Irving men, and a few others. (That is the gift of living and being raised by my father.) I can handle this. I answer his questions without swear words. We had dinner together, said our goodbyes.

Two weeks later, we were transferred back to Fredericton. After that, John's friends knew me as "Mrs Is-there-life-after-NO".

I was in a wee bit of Madness and used it wisely, for my own self-respect, my family, and myself. Sometimes we need to hang on, hang in, hang tight, but never hang up. NEVER. It is OUR life; no one else's. We may have to follow rules, but sometimes we need to bend them. We just do not need a drink to do so.

Fredericton, Oct 7, 1991: A new beginning, bittersweet

I am tired. God, I am so tired of this bullshit. I am tried of me, of thee, of us, the fuss.

I awoke at seven a.m. on Monday, October 7, 1991 and was so hungover that I didn't get the girls off to school. I heard them in the kitchen.

They left and John was not far behind them. It was the weekend of our sixteenth wedding anniversary. Our marriage was on the rocks. I didn't care, and I spent the weekend drinking and at a friend's house, partying. I arrived home to Starlite Village late Sunday afternoon. John was putting down slabs in our walkway. I said, "Hello."

No response. He didn't ask me where I'd been. He didn't care. (Well, I thought he didn't —it took me years to realize that he has a difficult time articulating his feelings.

I went in and downed more booze.

Monday morning felt different. I was so fed-up with myself; the shame, the self-loathing. Was it ever going to stop? I wrote a poem about it a few years later, which began with, "I woke up one morning with this in my head: *Your life is unraveling, now get out of bed."*

I literally yelled, "GOD HELP ME!" and plainly heard, "Call AA." So I did.

I remember going through the Yellow Pages and not being able to spell Alcoholics Anonymous. I was frustrated and heard, "Look up AA."

I made the call timidly and was told to meet a woman, Linda, in a downtown church basement at noon. The caller told me Linda would be wearing green pants with a black sweater. I looked down at myself—I had on a green sweater with black pants. *Okay, that's a sign.* That would be easy to remember. My head was pounding, but that voice I heard was louder than the pain in my head.

For some reason, in October 1991, I had on a fur coat. It must have been a cold fall. I was working for a local radio station and I left early to make my way to the meeting. Once I arrived, I sat on a bench opposite the church and watched the people entering. I was in a quandary. *Do I really belong with these people?* I heard that voice again. "Look behind you. If you do not walk through that door, you will end up there."

I turned my head. I was sitting in front of a graveyard. I slowly got up, walked across the street, and entered through those God forsaken doors.

My life would never be the same. It became bittersweet.

My days in AA lasted for ten years and I learned plenty about addiction; sugar, smoking, coffee, and relationship addictions. I heard it all. I stopped going to meetings after ten years as it became boring. All I heard was the Victim.

When people ask me where I have been, I tell them I am out living my life. What are they doing with theirs?

When I went home that day in October and told John and the girls at dinner that I did something different and joined AA. John said, "yes, that group is great for problem drinkers", my reply," No John, I am an Alcoholic".

Melanie was smart, the next day she went to her guidance counsellor and told them she did not want to live at home anymore and her mom was in AA.

The following Friday evening after John and I returned home from a hockey game, her room was empty. Her guidance counsellor found her an apartment, put her on welfare and while we were out of our house, helped her pack. In the province of New Brunswick you are considered an adult at 16. I was stepping into sobriety on a slippery slope.

She was in and out of her home, our house for the next four years.

Journey into the Twelve Steps

I awoke one morning with this in my head
"Awake this moment, now get out of bed,
Your life is unravelling, the chaos is clear,
Get yourself to a meeting, listen and hear.

1. You admit you are powerless over the liquid you choose; are you going to keep blaming? It is your life that you lose.
2. You admit a power greater than yourself; you have friends that are with you, I sent them to help.
3. You made a decision to give me your will; I am speaking to you—listen, be still.
4. Now is the step where you go deep within; look at yourself, be fearless, no sin.
5. You admitted your wrongs to me and yourself. Now it is time to confess to someone else.
6. You have the courage to do what it takes. I am removing your defects and your heartaches.
7. Being humbled, you started to feel. It is here you'll find wisdom; you're ready to heal.
8. Your amends there are many, too numerous to count. It is all in the past now, your guilt can't be found.
9. These memories are yours; no harm can be done. Let others "live and let live," their own lives have begun.
10. As you continue your journey, remember your light; when shadow advances, DO NOT ACCEPT and TAKE FLIGHT.

11. As you pray daily to me and yourself, deep into your meditation is where I do dwell.
12. This awakening is not yours to keep—Go out, speak truth, help those who still weep.

(Lilly White)

REMEMBER that day you awoke without aid.

Beauty and the Beast

The only thing worse than being bipolar, is being beautiful or handsome and having a mental illness. No one wants to believe you are NOT okay. You are cunning, baffling, and brilliant. You walk into a room and you take everyone's breathe away. Your blond hair, workout body, and creamy, dewy complexion say, "I am together in mind, body and spirit." Everyone judges you by your cover. But what is buried deep underneath?

This was our daughter Melanie from the age of twelve until her death at thirty-seven.

She had been to the doctors; they diagnosed her at thirty-one. Before that, all her issues belonged to someone else. Us (her parents), her friends, her lovers, her teachers. I do not hold many regrets but one of them is that I did not know Melanie was ill. I thought she was just rebellious. I was a child raising a child and wanted to make her see right from wrong. I did not understand she was incapable of understanding my words or actions. I did not abuse her physically, but I surely did emotionally. Together we were dancing the dance of anger. We two stepped around each other, tripped many times, and waltzed out of each other's lives for years.

She wanted all the privileges of adulthood but none of the responsibility. And she could charm anyone. They took one look at her and were smitten. She had amazing survival skills and was brilliant at planning, scheming, and organizing. Whatever she said was gospel to anyone who did not know her. To those of us who did know her, trust was an issue. We saw through her. Looks and charm did not work on us, and we paid the price, many times over. That beast inside of her, that she or anyone else could not control, was an illness that reaped what it sowed. She suffered, and everyone around her suffered. The beast would not tell her when it was going to make an entrance. Some days she was subtle; most days she was shrewd. She would con a con; steal from a thief, set fire to a blaze. The next story is an example.

David who?

June 17, 1992—a beautiful Friday morning. John was happily off to work, Amanda to school. Melanie was driving to Port Elgin to pick up her date for her graduation, Rainer. It was nine a.m. and I was reading one of my favourite authors at the time, Gary Zukav—a book called *Seat of the Soul*.

The phone rang. "Hello, may I speak to Melanie please?"

"No," I reply, "she is away at the moment. Can I help you?"

"Yes, this is David. Melanie has asked me to her prom dance and I need to know the colour of her dress so I can buy her a corsage. Should I get one for her arm or one to be pinned on her dress?"

In that moment, I didn't know if I should laugh or cry. I had never heard of this David, and Melanie had just taken our vehicle to travel three hours from Fredericton to Port Elgin to pick up her date for the prom.

If you can, I want you to imagine this: Be me for a minute. Do you tell this guy he has the wrong number? Do you tell him the colour of Mel's dress? Maybe you are brave and tell him that she has also invited someone else whom she is travelling at this very minute to pick up? It is moments like this that you feel NUTS. You are losing your marbles.

Shit, it was only nine a.m. for heavens/soul's sake (as Gary Z would say). *What the fudge do I say? Breathe in...* "David," I said, "I am so grateful you called—it is with regret that I tell you she has another date for this evening."

"Oh, I do not think that is possible," was his reply.

I realized that this was not my issue. I was not going to buy the bait and get hooked. I released the tightness in my chest and stomach. Once again I breathed in and said, "Okay, her dress is periwinkle blue."

"Thank you," and he hung up.

When Melanie and her date arrived I mentioned the phone call. She denied any knowledge of this David person. I was too tired to argue, plus her date was with us. Also, I had to keep reminding myself this was not my drama. She will handle it. It was not spoken of again.

Listen to your gut; your gut has a brain

It was a long day...

It was 1993. I had just returned home from working as a sales executive with CFNB in Fredericton. I was tired, but family came first so I picked up a few groceries on the way home to make dinner. When I arrived at our home in Starlite Village, there was a car there that I did not recognize.

Upon entering, I saw Amanda was in the kitchen doing her homework. John was just coming through the door at the same time as me, and Melanie and a friend were downstairs. She introduced us to her friend, but I cannot remember his name right now. It doesn't matter. Immediately all my cells went cold, my back went up, and my brain went crazy with dizziness. After the introductions, I went upstairs to brush my teeth. Why brushing my teeth was so important at that moment I do not care to remember, but I said to John, "GET THAT YOUNG MAN OUT OF OUR HOUSE!"

John's response: "There you go again, acting crazy. Why do you do this? Why don't you give her a chance? Why do you always think the worst?"

"It's a feeling," I tried to explain. "I do not like how I feel." I looked around the bathroom, seeing the tub, the floor, the colour of blue; everything seemed so much bigger, brighter. *Maybe I am losing my mind? Maybe I should calm down. John is right, I am making a big deal out of nothing.*

I made supper and we all sat down together. He told us his story; that he was living in Saint John and had a good job, and about how he and Melanie met. Great—end of evening, he left. I was relieved.

Within a month, Melanie had moved in with him.

I was offended—she was only in her late teens but continued to tell me that in New Brunswick she was considered an adult. I settled into acceptance. Loving her—that was all that was important. I accepted her, not her decision.

It was three months later, two a.m. The phone rang. John answered; the phone was next to him this night. It was a police officer from Saint John.

I listened to John say, "Yes, mmm hmm, yes… We will be there in an hour. Is she okay?" He hung up.

I was holding my breath. *What now?*

John told me, "That guy you don't like? He beat the living daylights out of her. She is in the hospital. You didn't like him…How could I have not heard?" he asked me.

"Jesus, John," was my reply. "Why can't you feel things instead of thinking? Your gut has a brain—use it."

She was pressing charges. She had the strength of a warrior goddess. She went to court on her own. She didn't want us anywhere near the courtroom, as there were things only for her ears. We respected her decision, but it was not easy to do so. The young man was charged with abuse and given one year in jail to be served on weekends. She was pleased with the verdict and was onto another relationship. This time she moved in with a friend of hers from Cadets. She told us he was gay. We had met him at hospital, when she was there with her bruises from her young man, whom I did not like. This new one is a darling of a man. They moved in together into a small, comfortable apartment in Saint John. For a few months I thought all was well.

One afternoon, I received another phone call. Her "roommate" had a question to ask me. He was confused about their sex life and thought I could help.

Confused? Suddenly, it was me who was confused. "What are you talking about? Melanie told us you were gay."

"What?" was his reply? "No, I am not. Why would she say that?"

My sense is it was due to the shame she felt from her abusive boyfriend and the idea of telling us she was moving in with another mate so soon…I think she was afraid of our judgment.

Melanie had amazing survival skills and was brilliant. But not being able to trust or to be trustworthy can lead to Madness.

Remember this was 1993. I tried many times to connect over the phone to doctors in Ontario to explain to them that something was off with our daughter. Nothing was heard or understood. Bipolar disorder was not well known during the early nineties.

Angels' grace, Amanda's gifts

Here is an insane story of how I could have hurt my daughter Amanda while thinking I was helping her. My own madness.

My God, can the weather be any colder? It was November 23, 1993. Amanda and I had moved into a small trailer on Hanson Rd. in Fredericton. I had left John for a few months. When I walked out the door it was one day at a time.

Everything in my life was "Just for today…" It was the only way I could survive.

That cold, brisk morning while I was in the trailer, the motor had died in my car, the pipes in the trailer were frozen, and the mice were settling in for the winter. With all of this there was still calmness between Amanda and me. We were free from the chaos for a while.

There was, however, one issue that kept going through my mind over and over; finances for university. Amanda was going to be starting university soon. She was currently attending a French school; not immersion, but Ecole St. Ann. One of her parents was supposed to have been French for her to attend, but she was very fluent in French, so they had enrolled her. Our daughter has a brilliant mind. University was two years away and I did not know how we were going to pay for it.

A crazy thought went through my head. By the grace of God, it did not enter my heart and I did not act upon it. "Chakra bypass," I call it. I had an insurance policy of $150,000, which I had taken out on myself some years ago. I wondered if something happened to me, if that would be enough to pay for her university.

She left for school, and as I sat in the kitchen, next to the door, listening to the howl of the wind on that cold day, I realized I could help her. I began to feel depressed at the thought of leaving her and everyone, but life had been such a struggle. *Who would miss me anyway?* Amanda? She was young and she'd survive. She'd still have John and Melanie. John? He must have been fed up with me. Melanie? That was not likely.

As I sat with my head in my hands, the phone rang. It was my AA sponsor, wanting to know if I would like to go for a coffee and shopping. She had a few items to pick up. I figured it would be a good opportunity to say my goodbyes, so I agreed and told her I would be ready in an hour.

The day turned into a day of laughter and joy. When Linda dropped me off at the trailer, I was in a better state of mind and not so heavy. I thought to myself, *I will deal with Amanda's university another day.*

Amanda ended up receiving scholarships for both her MA and her PhD. Can you imagine if Linda had not called that day? My Martyr, thinking I was helping Amanda, would have brought about such a catastrophe! My life would have been short; my death would have been long… into eternity.

Daily there is grace surrounding us. We are not aware of it at the time. Angels are everywhere in the form of people, places, and things. We have to awaken to them.

It was from this experience that I finally surrendered—the beginnings of hope. I surrendered and began to study. I studied with Doreen Virtue, Caroline Myss, Dr. Mario Martinez. I found new tools to be awake to my higher self. I found ways to know and love myself, but not before a dark night of the soul

Note: HOPE = Helping Others Pray & Play Every day.

I SURRENDER

I was still living in a small trailer with Amanda. John had been asking me to return home. "Not without help and advice from a counsellor," I replied. In January 1994, he agreed. Both of us were willing to work on our individual issues, as well as our issues as a couple.

One evening, John suggested to Melanie that she leave. She would not take responsibility for her credit cards and her spending. He had found another $400 of clothes in her closet. (The apple does not fall far from the tree; She was a mirror of me). She would not pay him board and continued to spend. She continued to blame everyone else and point the finger at others. John's denial was finally coming off.

These issues were the ones I'd run from when I'd left our home in Starlite Village. I was tired of the daily struggles, the fighting, and the finger pointing. This energy was not going to help keep me sober, plus it was a toxic environment for Amanda. She was always the watcher and she had witnessed enough.

One cold day, I awoke to the freezing pipes in the trailer, yet with an inner sense of calm. *I am not going to allow anyone to take this feeling from me*. Melanie was suicidal because her dad had requested for her to leave. She was nineteen. My marriage was on the rocks, I was in debt, I had no job, the motor was gone on my car, mice were in the trailer, and the pipes were frozen. Extraordinarily, however, I was calm. I realized that change is pain. However, if it is for our growth, it is not so difficult. I was there in that trailer and I loved the silence. In a few months after John and I entered counselling, Amanda and I moved back home to Starlite Village.

The wind howls,
the snow drifts,
another season,
without reason,
change.

By 1994 I was able to look at every day as a gift; to accept the light and the shadow and know that somewhere deep within—all is a lesson. We only get what is needed for our growth. If I expect NO thing, EVERY thing is a bonus.

If I can be calm this day,
calm will say, "Come forth, I will hold you."
I SURRENDER.

Merciful God

It was Monday, April 19, 1994. I was so excited for Melanie, but I was also very angry. *Am I going crazy in my late thirties?*

She has won the Duke of Edinburgh Award. She had passed many exams with the cadet core, was promoted to lieutenant at a very early age and was a mentor to many of her peers. Prince Edward from England was coming to Fredericton to present her with award. We were over the top with excitement at the supper table. We were hearing this news, but something was not right within me. I felt it but was unaware of what it was.

Two weeks went by. I was looking for my skies but couldn't find them. Melanie had moved out once again. She was home for the weekend and this time, when she left, she took what she wanted. This was a habit of hers. No boundaries, no asking, just taking. I tried to understand; I guessed it was my fault. I thought if I didn't get angry with her so often, perhaps she would tell me things; ask for her needs to be met instead of taking. She was always taking; energetically and physically. The awards. I would not go. Everyone was in shock. So was I. I didn't understand, but I was grounded, paralyzed, couldn't move. I couldn't go, even if I willed myself to go.

John was angry. He didn't understand, and I couldn't explain. He and Amanda left to pick up Melanie. Three hours later they arrived home. In those three hours I had been to hell and back. I was a bad mother; I was filled with shame. *What the fudge is the matter with me?* John's words upon arriving home: "Thank God one of us was there—it would have looked bad."

BINGO. I had won the lottery. I immediately understand why I could not go. To show up for appearances' sake is not a reason for support. Melanie had won this award, but not without a crucifixion of us. We had been nailed to the cross many times. We had watched her lie, steal, and take, with no consequences. The law was on her side. The parents were the problem and in New Brunswick, children of sixteen-plus are considered adults unless they kill someone…and then it is back on the parents again.

To show up to celebrate her when she was so disruptive, distortive, would not have not been right. It would have been a sham, showing up because of what people thought. If I was to teach her anything, it was not that. I had to stand my ground.

Until the day she died, she thought I did not care. I cared very much. We loved her deeply, but saying one thing and living another was not teaching her anything. I am left to wonder if perhaps it would have been the right thing to go. Go; sit up in the front with a smile; the mask, and pretend once again. At least she would have had the memory of me being there instead of an impression that I did not care. I did care and if I knew then what I know today about mental illness I would have understood and possibly gone to the ceremony. As I write this sadness is overwhelming. I weep for all of us who do not understand mental illness.

Sometimes you cannot take back your actions. You fess up and take the responsibility for causing others pain, even at the expense of truth. There is no cost to love. Only a debt to the soul when you have gambled the possibilities of unconditional love.

If I had known what I know now, if I had more information about her disease, I would have been in the front row applauding her—for her, not for show and tell. I would have forgiven her stealing the skies, her lying and understood she knew not what she did.

Study this disease, donate to mental health, and find out everything you can. It may save someone life.

The mole on our shoulders

I am not sure where I heard this phrase, but it is intriguing: "Mental illness is real. It is like a mole on our shoulder we do not take seriously. It stays with us in the subtlest of ways. Suddenly, it is bleeding and no one can fix it. It is beyond repair."

I like to think of myself as an optimist, and those who truly know me would agree. I will take lemons and create something sweet; I will walk down the fearful path because I know I am not alone. I believe. However, when it comes to mental illness in our society, I am lost.

I took a doctor on a trip—a spiritual journey—and because a dear friend had recommended this woman, when I interviewed her in preparation for the trip, I overlooked a few of her comments. She was a doctor—who was I to question? (That in itself shows the level of my self-worth. Its nuts.)

When we arrived at our destination, it was clear this person was ill. She was filled to the gills with booze and prescription drugs. Upon arrival, while we sat at a table discussing our trip with the tour guide, this person was in bed, passed out. By the grace of God/Goddess I had three other people on that trip in a twelve-step program, so we all knew how to handle this kind of situation. It was not easy. As soon as this individual had a drink, there was a scene. She would become loud and obnoxious. In those ten days, whenever we had dinner and she had a glass of wine, we crossed our fingers and rolled our eyes. Whenever she was challenged, her reply? "I am a doctor, I will take you down. You will never work again." Power. The want of it is an addiction and in the mentally ill category, in my humble opinion.

What in the name of all that is holy is the problem with us and our society that we do not recognize mental illness until it is too late?

Take for example, your child of seventeen years. He or she is in the first year of university. That was our Melanie in 1992. She was starting on her journey into a scholastic future. What happened? There were banks in the corridors of her university offering credit cards. She did not have a job; she was living with us once again. Within three months she owed money. What is wrong with this picture? Are we going to say, "Oh, it is our society and that's the way it is," or are we going to say "ENOUGH!?" This is crazy-making. *What will happen when she is out of university?* I can tell you a story, but that is another chapter, before she took her life, when she declared bankruptcy. She felt her life was in ruins. Yes, I realize that she made the decisions but really, asking a seventeen-year-old if she wants a credit card is like telling a bear at a dumpster to sit down and wait while I serve him. Duh—he will attack.

Our Doctor friend and our Melanie are mirror images on myself.

The dark night of the soul

Saint John of God, a Catholic mystic in the sixteenth century, first wrote this about. His poem narrates the journey of the soul from its bodily home to its union with God. The journey is called "The Dark Night," because darkness represents the hardships and difficulties the soul meets in detachment from the world and in reaching the light of the union with the Creator. (WIKI)

There have been many books written about this union, this journey, but until you experience your own path, all books, teachings may elude you. You may even find yourself running or escaping the pathway to your inner mystic. You may say things like: I do not believe in darkness. I will work on manifesting, being happy. I will not allow darkness to penetrate me. This friend is your ego.

Many seekers would encourage the dark-night experience if they knew what it was. The road to our higher consciousness will pass through a dark night.

A higher consciousness is not wanting more of something; more money, more happiness, more love. It is a deep yearning, a merging or unity with the higher self. It may feel like a sacred initiation with the Divine and yes, this is exactly what it is. The dark night is a very private matter. You will feel alone. You are alone in your ego, but in the space of your spirit, your soul, activity is happening. Your dreams are vivid, nature is talking, your body is screaming, your brain is fried. You may feel exhausted. The dark night will push you into a hole of sorts to make sure you are still in your body and now ready to just be with spirit. (Be sure to read about my journey into the rabbit hole.)

The dark night may begin with your house burning down, the death of a loved one, a red bank balance or simply a lack of energy to give to or care about yourself or anyone else. A dark night can last for a few months or a few years. We can have more than one in this lifetime or have one that lasts a lifetime. *Mother Teresa of Calcutta, according to letters released in 2007, "may be the most extensive such case on record," lasting from 1948 almost up until her death in 1997, with only brief interludes of relief in between. [WIKI)*

Peace comes with acceptance; an understanding that we are not alone. Others have followed this journey and they have an inner knowing that God is leading them deeper into themselves.

I love what Caroline Myss wrote to me a few months ago. "At some point, a person has to pause and realize that only Heaven could so empty one's life so completely. Only Heaven could create a life path that intersects with the release of the lives of others so dear to them in a simultaneous way."

I first wrote about this dark night in 2010, a year before all the losses. This has been my third dark night in this lifetime. I consider myself blessed to continue on this sacred journey and I will continue to dive deeper into consciousness. It is not an easy path, but one I take with joy and compassion. The joy allows me to live an adventure each day and compassion allows me to be gentle with myself. I allow myself to feel sorrow, to understand, to stop judgment. To BE, to simply BE.

In 1994 I remember a day the dark night was once again upon me. The girls were getting ready for school; Melanie was home again for a time. There was a huge fight about something or other and I drove John to work as Melanie had the car. Upon arriving home to Starlite Village, 116 Taurus drive, I drove right into the garage, shut the door, and left the car running. I was not thinking, I was to damn angry. I was fed up. I was not depressed—I was in a rage. I started to fall asleep but heard, *you realize you will have to come back and do this again until you get it right.*

I jumped up and responded, "Get what right? I am fed up with me, the family, my life." Suddenly the anger left and a warm feeling came over me from the tips of my toes to my neck. I was flushed, warm, and at peace. I turned the car off, went inside and called my AA sponsor, Linda. She was a nurse and when I told her what I had done she came and picked me up. She brought me to her home for a few days and explained that the flush and now my nausea were signs the fumes were poisoning me. I felt ashamed of myself but as usual Linda did not judge me.

Most people think that suicide is depression, but I have witnessed where it can also be triggered by anger and rage. That insanity we feel when we are powerless. My brother was angry when he took his life. He left us a tape with all the reasons why. Melanie was angry with her beloved and with good reason but that was no reason to leave us. She drove her car away from her home so her children would not look for her in the house. She walked home, went downstairs, took a scarf, and that was her end.

Mental illness has many faces. Uncontrolled anger is just one of them.

A Poem I wrote in 2010.

Dark Night of My Soul.

Been down this road so many times, on my knees looking for my last dime.
In this state, my heart was heavy, but here I surrendered and I felt ready.
Ready for what I did not know but I stopped looking and ask spirit to show,
Show me the path I had not taken, a dark night
of my soul, there was no mistaken.
The anger, the shame, the disappointment of self,
I am on my knees I needed no help.
For here my mind is free of confusion, my liberty, no longer an illusion.
I entertain silence, this space of loudness, the deafen-
ing sound of my ego that is parted.
I gather all that I am or all that has resigned herself…
to a perfect love, a blind faith, pure hope and abandoned trust.
For this, to love you deeply God…I must…I must
Then this dark night of my soul becomes the Holy
Grail that allows me to be whole.

Another example of Madness

July 1st, 1996.

I was so excited I could hardly stand it. Ottawa called. In one of my previous chapters you have read of how that almost did not come to pass. John and I were now together after many appointments with a counsellor. Melanie was not the issue, WE WERE.

We accepted and integrated into our being.

We were happy and looking forward to a new lease on life. Amanda was beginning university at UNB, with honours. Melanie was working at Bell Canada in Saint John, NB and all appeared well.

Fudge and double fudge, another phone call.

"Hi, is this Mrs. White?"

Whenever I heard these words, I wanted say, "No, this is Miss Black and my room is in the back." But alas, I was married and had two girls and had to behave myself and not hide.

"Yes," I slowly replied, wanting time to stand still for I intuitively knew this was trouble.

This moment was going to change everything, every fudge thing, AGAIN.

"This is Lee, I have been with Melanie now for a few months."

"Yes, Lee, she has spoken of you, especially last week when we went to visit her in Saint John."

"I need to tell you something," he said.

I did not want to hear it for I had heard this before, and I did not want any more like before.

"Melanie and I have been having troubles and she is now pregnant and did it on purpose so she could move to Ottawa with you."

PREGNANT, God, how I hate that word, can we please say, she is expecting, she is with child? PREGNANT is so HUGE and final. "Thank you for calling, Lee," was all I could manage.

On July second, Melanie came for a visit.

She told us her news, which we were already privy to but we did not tell her for it would betray Lee.

She sat there, hostile, as if we owed her something—*I am going with you to Ottawa, I am in a mess and you HAVE to take me with you.*

She was in her bedroom, her bedroom she had not been in for a few years but we had kept for her to return to when needed.

Now we were leaving, the house was sold and we were out of there July 15th. This room would belong to someone else.

As she lay her head down, I explained that she was almost twenty-two, and she had made her decisions in life. Now it was time for her to grow up and accept her fate. Any choices made now would lead to her destiny.

The next day she was angry with us. It was her power struggle within herself. She could not believe we were actually leaving her. Her control had always been that she was leaving US.

She once again threatened to take her life. This was her seventh time in her twenty-two years of wanting to end her life. Many a time we picked her up at the hospital. Today she left us in chaos.

For the first time in our twenty-two years together I saw John break down and cry. We didn't know what to do but we got in our vehicle and left for Ottawa. It was like a honeymoon that we never had.

The next time I saw him cry was fifteen years later when she was dead. We were at a restaurant in Moncton, NB.

It was myself, John, Amanda, Mark, (Amanda's husband's) and our wee one-year-old Tatiana. We were eating lunch. Melanie's funeral was the next day. Amanda made the comment that it was strange that Melanie gave her youngest child Xavier who was five, the last name of White instead of his father's last name, Gallagher.

"No," I answered, "she told me that she wanted to honour her dad. She said that Xavier was the only boy in our family, and she loved her father so much she wanted the White name to carry on."

John wept.

PATTERNS and Details

One such detail I was oblivious to was Melanie's' school report. Recently, I went looking for Amanda's baptism certificate. She was in need of it to enrol one of her girls in daycare. I did not think anything of the task until I began shifting through years of documents. I had not realized that even with all the transfers and moves we'd had, when it came to school documents I had kept everything. I took the time to review Melanie's. (A bitter-sweet experience). I planned to get her school reports in some type of order so her children could have them if they so desired. I was stunned as I shifted through each document. Grade one to ten; the teachers' remarks were all the same. "Melanie is a good student." "Melanie needs to learn to focus and not be so active." "Melanie is too scattered.

Each year she would come home, I would look at her A-B grades, congratulate her and think to myself, *Oh, those teachers, they are just not fast enough for her. Not for my clever girl.*

However, when she was home she was tired, sulky, and rarely smiled. I was very young at the time and didn't realize the reports did not register the difference in her mood swings. That did not come into my consciousness until she left us when she was sixteen.

She was in and out for four tremulous years. It was at this time, John and I went into counselling to ask for direction, guidelines, suggestions, anything to help us deal with her behaviour.

We tend to think that everything will go away. Tomorrow will be a better day. We are living the best way we know how and that this is normal. The mood swings, the lying, the anger, the blaming, the tears, the panic, the chaos, this is all normal.

This is NOT normal, these are patterns.

Patterns—recognize them for what they are. Yes, seek help, either for yourselves to deal with the crazies or for your loved one.

Mental illness will not go away. Unfortunately the person may leave, die, or emotionally shut down.

Watch the patterns, the details. Witness the sequences of sadness, madness. They have a story to tell.

I have been watching our billing patterns with Bell, don't even get me started on that. "Let's talk about it," their campaign for mental illness. Bell will drive us crazy with $11.000.00 phone bills and their poor communication skills. Will they talk about that? I think not. Society lives in patterns and thinks it is normal.

When we bring something into being we become Co Creators with the Universe.

In 2008 I heard Desmond Tutu at the Quest for Global Healing tell us, "You are all God Creators, now go Create God." Powerful words.

At our daughter's funeral in 2012, her dad, John gave a list of her accomplishments; a list of what she had created in her thirty-seven short years. She had been an interior decorator, a fire fighter, a police officer, a business owner, A Duke of Edinburgh recipient, a mother, and a wife, to name but a few examples of what she had created for herself and others. She also suffered from mental illness. She was diagnosed as bipolar five years before her death by suicide. John and I had been aware of problems since she was twelve, but at that time we thought it was normal for teenagers to act the way she had, no matter how extreme the behaviour.

She was continually attempting to bring something into existence. Bringing forth what she did not see but knew existed in the heavens.

Isn't that what being creative is? Bringing down from the heavens the God source in form? We forever want closeness, a oneness with the source and we attain that when we are allowing the juices of our passions, our creativity, to have us.

We want to experience Heaven on Earth. We desire to get closer to the beloved. We feel this intimacy when we love what we do, when we breathe in the creative source and give it form.

It can come through as painting, poetry, architecture, policing, writing, athletics, cooking, style, yoga, dance, and much more. All this imaginative power can be very healing.

Once we stop creating we will no longer need to meet God, we have united with this source. Much like Buddha, Jesus, and Muhammad. We will be free to sit and just BE in peace. We will teach what we know, just as they did. We become one with divinity.

For some of us there is certain madness when in the process of creating. If not balanced, creating can lead us into temptation, into a feeling of self-doubt. We may sabotage our creations; find out there is no road leading us out of our crazies. There are many instances of this throughout history. Van Gogh, Hemingway, Sylvia Plath, and Virginia Woolf are just a few examples. Edgar Allan Poe died a mysterious death and some say his last words were, "Lord, help my poor soul."

There are numerous ways to experience balance while we are being co-creators. I have listed a few at the end of this book.

SUCIDE is never the answer to, "how do we find balance?"

July 4th, 2000

John had just left for work, via his bicycle. It was a gorgeous day and I had a few appointments with Crabtree accounts.

It was Wednesday. The previous weekend one of my brothers and his family were in Ottawa visiting us. We had the opportunity to meet his new bride-to-be. Between them they had eight children. All was well, or so I thought.

The phone rang. That damn phone again.

It was nine a.m. Funny how you remember the day, that time, that exact moment when life stands still, and all is in slow motion. *God, why are the birds singing?* You ask yourself as your sister says through her crying voice, "Lillian, we have lost Derek."

What are you talking about? I just left him a phone message last evening to sing him happy birthday. I was not in town for his birthday on the 26th of June and forgot over the weekend while our other brother was here. "What do you mean we lost him?" I repeated.

Through her sobs I was able to understand what she was crying about: "Derek has hung himself. God, oh God," she repeats. "Why?"

My first questions to her were, "How? Where?" And then, "How are Mom and Dad?"

My family used to live in Alberta; Fort McMurray to be exact. The place where saltwater cowboys live. That's what they called Newfoundlanders who moved there. My family had been residing in that town since 1978. It is also known as Fort McMoney.

I needed the logistics of what I was hearing from her. I was too dumb or numb, I am not sure but I did not want to feel this. There were only eighteen months between Derek and me. I, being the oldest, left home at barely nineteen years old. I loved him, but we were not close enough to understand or talk about each other's pain or difficulties. I do remember him coming into my bedroom on October 4th, 1974 as I was changing from my wedding dress to put on my dress for the reception. I remember him telling me how happy he was for me and that John was a great guy. I remember how sad I felt for him that he had to stay there in that house. I remember him calling me when I was in a trailer in 1995. He was the only one in my family who knew I had left John for a few months. I recall him giving me courage.

Courage was something Derek had plenty of but it was unbeknownst to him. The last time I saw him was July 1998. John and I had taken a trip out west, flew into Calgary, rented a car and drove to BC. Our last day of holiday, we were at the park in Didsbury which Mom and Dad looked after for the summer months.

Derek was there camping with his trailer, something he loved; camping, nature, and cowboy hats. That was our Derek. That morning before we left for the airport I went to say goodbye to my brother. Little did I know it was to be my last goodbye. As I was kissing him farewell, I said, "My God Derek, you look like you are in such physical pain."

His reply: "Lillian, I am always in pain."

It was in that moment; that flash as the sun was rising; the scent of dew on the grass; the bird to my left that I finally understood his drinking. It hit with such a bolt that I started to cry. He thought I was crying because I did not want to leave, I was crying that I had been unable to see.

Derek was born with one leg longer than the other and a curve in his spine; scoliosis. I have mini scoliosis. Something else that runs in the family.

His courage when he was a child, from my point of view, made him a hero. He was always in braces of some kind and frequently making trips to St John's hospital. One time he had a plaster cast from his chest down.

I think he was around ten years of age at that time. Remember, we were children but from my child's prospective, I cannot ever remember him complaining. EVER. My other siblings, I am sure they would have their own story and perspective.

I do however remember his anger. When he was young his anger was not outward, but there was always something I could see and feel but could not identity. I wrote about it years later in a journal. I wrote how he and Melanie had a similar energy about them. Now I know it was inner anger not expressing itself. It would have been a slow burn inside of them, their low self-worth, and low self-esteem. It was a fire waiting to ignite. It was not a coincidence that they both took their lives in the same way—hanging.

Hanging on to things, not feeling free to express and if they did because of their anger, nobody would listen.

I remember him mowing the lawn, dragging his foot. Dad was not going to raise him any differently than the rest of us so he had chores also. In fact, I was usually protecting him when possible, but when it came to household chores Dad had the upper hand. My recollection is our brother Al helping Derek out when possible. Now Derek is gone, no one can help him.

There is much guilt and remorse from all of us, his siblings. He was the one who suffered more than the rest of us. He was the one with the physical pain as well as the emotional pain. We are not sure as to why on the day of his funeral we were confused and lost. There were no words. We had lost a limb from our tree. Perhaps if we'd had the physical aliments as he did we would have gone also. It was all too much to bear. Our father was there, confused also, and our mom seemed angry and in her own pain. Dad was upset with her and told her it would be okay.

No it is not okay. You are not aware of what is really happening, Dad. You are unable to understand the damage. For then you will have to look at yourself.

Maybe Derek sacrificed himself for us. Maybe at some level he understood the illness in our family and could not go on with the way life was. We will never know. I know this though. I had a dream a month after Derek's death. Maybe the dream was so real because Derek had left us a tape of his last hour, blaming his suicide on the hospital, the banks, the government and a few other things. We actually heard him hanging himself in the tape; the moving of the chair and then dark silence.

In my dream I see Derek put the rope around his neck, climb the chair next to the banister, and drop. But in the dream I am him and I see grey matter when I actually die and hear myself say, "Oops." *Now what? This is real. I can no longer exist as me. I am now everyone and the awareness is overwhelming. I have to go back to make amends. This was a mistake. I want to go back.*

The energy next to me says, "Not yet. You will stay here and help others; we have a huge amount of work to do.

"Good," I say, "At least I am no longer in physical pain." But oh, the pain now of feeling the agony of those I have left behind. I am shown it takes generations to heal.

I am filled once again with sorrow but the energy next to me says, "Stop. Get to work. There are others on their way, no one is learning from your departure."

I awake confused, I am Lilly again but Derek is with me for a very long time.

Suicide is never the answer or solution to what ails us. Yes, we enter a hole, a dark night of our souls, but to leave this planet without allowing the natural law of the universe to unfold is self-slaying. We slay ourselves and the lives of those we leave behind. We are part of a family, even if we are unable to feel it. If we do not have an intimate family, we are part of the family of humanity. We are here for a reason.

To evolve.

Not to slaughter ourselves and make those we leave behind revolve and go backwards with the pain of loss again, again, and again.

In 2012 Melanie took her life in the same way as my brother. A hanging. Within a week I had a dream:

Once again, I am her and I am putting the scarf around my neck. *Damn this life and all those who cause me pain* is my last thought. I feel the tightness on my neck, then darkness. My last breath is not painful but filled with anger. I hear myself say "OOPS," this is for real. I cannot go back. I am still feeling angry; nothing has changed. I was supposed to change, now what? *Can I go back?*

"No," says a familiar energy, "you have work to do. No one has learnt anything from your departure."

I awoke and my daughter's energy hung around me for many months. I was filled with remorse.

Remorse to Redemption

In 2001 John was posted to Kosovo for nine months with the RCMP and the UN. At that time we were living in Orleans, Ontario. I was working for Crabtree & Evelyn and busy with my business Whitelight and the Trinity Table. At my business Whitelight I was coaching clients through the tools of Angels and I had purchased the Trinity Table. A five hundred pounds of sold oak table that spins 4 spins per minute. With eyes closed and the vibration of music you are brought into an awareness of deep relaxation. Here in Theta is were we begin to heal. Jim Harmon in Texas originally developed the table for drugs and alcoholics to bring them into peace and meditation.

I was in meditation one morning on this table in my Angel/Fairy room when I felt a presence hovering around me. I asked who it was and saw a vision with a name, "Tatiana." She was delightful and said she would be the communicator between John and me while he was away. Internet was not so great then although I do have nine months of emails I hope to share with our grandchildren one day. Tatiana, this fairy, said that any information I wanted to share with John I could give to her while I was in prayer and she would transfer the information to him. Perfect. Just what I needed to feel close to him during our time apart. Each morning during meditation or prayer in my Angel room I would send him thoughts, love, and ADVICE. (LOL).

I did this regularly. In July of 2005, I was visiting our daughter Amanda in Spain for a month. She was finishing up her PhD and living in Lugo, Spain for a year. One evening, I told her I needed to go to an Internet cafe to email her dad. By 2005 he was doing another UN mission, this time in East Timor. While we were having coffee, I mentioned that Tatiana had given me a message I needed to give to John. Amanda's face went white. "Mom, where did you get that name?" she asked.

"Oh in prayer. Our guardian, who sends us messages, that is her name," I replied.

Amanda then proceeded to tell me that ever since she could remember she had decided that if she had a daughter, she would name her Tatiana. Do-do, we both had goose bumps.

The years passed. John had seven missions in total. (Kosovo, East Timor, Afghanistan, and four in Haiti.)

The day arrived when Amanda announced that she is expecting. I sensed this was John's last mission. And so it was.

A week before Tatiana was born, a few friends and I were at Amanda's baby shower. Someone asked what she would name the baby. Her reply was, "I am not sure, but if it is a girl, Mark, my husband, likes the name Tatiana. But that is Mom's thing."

I thought she had forgotten by then what she told me in Spain. One of the attendees at the shower decided to look in the baby book for the meaning of names, LOL, Tatiana means "Fairy Queen" in Russian. Wonders of Wonder.

Amanda said, "We will know her name when we see her."

May 19th, 2011 arrived. A baby girl was born. An hour into her first day here on earth, now her new home, her new mommy, Amanda, called out a few names. She did not open her eyes. Then, softly, ever so softly, Amanda whispered, "Tatiana, Tatiana." A moment in silence, heartbeats slowed down, breathing was lowered, a hush fell over them, eyes opened and baby and mother's souls united. Yes, she now had her name.

Tatiana was a joy to all. At two years old, she called me Fairy Lilly and John, her grandpa, she called MONKA. That was all she called him: "Where is Monika?" or "Where is my Monika?" and my favourite, "See you soon, Monika." She adores him.

We wondered why she called him MONKA. Today I searched, yes in Kosovo, Monika is Monk.

John has eight archetypes exclusive to him: "the jester, knight, athlete, father, doubter, and yes, you guessed it, the MONK.

So, if you do not believe in fairies, look back into your life, there is a story waiting to be told. Just for today, let your magical story have you. Believe in YOU, believe in NOW, believe in WOW. It can redeem us.

Redemption To Forgiveness

In April of 2012, I received a call from Harpo Studios, from lovely women by the name of M.

"Hello, is Lilly White available? This is M from Harpo Studios."

Who does not want to hear these words?

I was at my store, the White Lilly, and M was calling me regarding a question I had emailed earlier that morning. It was a question I hoped that Deepak could answer.

They had asked if we were living our passion and had any forgiveness issues we were working on. *Yes, I do, I am living my passion but not my highest potential, how do I know? I am sick all the time since I opened the store. Something is out of whack. I am taking what others say personally and this is not how I expected I would react.*

After all, the store had been opened just as Spirit instructed me. Bring my love of Bali home instead of John and I retiring there.

When M asked how this related to forgiveness, I replied that if we do not take people, places, or things personally, there is nothing to forgive.

Great, she gave me instructions what to do when I was in Toronto.

I was on my way, excited. Imagine, I had a change to be on Oprah—going to be amazing for BUSINESS.

I arrived, met a staff member, and was told that NO the question would not be asked. I had answered it myself. M's question , "What is forgiveness"? My answer, "If we take nothing personally , where is nothing to forgive" . When I spoke to M it was mostly related to my business. Right church-wrong pew.

Within the first hour, Bishop Jakes was telling us that we could be anything or do anything we gave birth to. We were pregnant…

I almost fainted in my chair, I was dizzy, confused, and then bang, right to the heart, Diana my staff member asked me if I was OK. I could only hear Spirit: *Your business was a replacement for the fact that you have been estranged from your daughter for twenty years. You continue to give birth. Power up your life. Breakfast with Soul, the White Lilly, Mayan Study group, Soul journeys to Bali and much more. God forbid that anyone should judge your achievements; they are attacking your motherhood.*

I had been out there doing instead of sitting still. Instead of loving and knowing that when my daughter was ready, (it might take thirty years.) but she would come eventually. Or she might not. Yes, I have made my amends to her, she has not yet accepted them but I do not need to substitute for her by DOING and finding new ways to give birth.

I accepted and surrendered to the fact that she was unable to forgive me, but I had not yet surrendered to this pain; the pain of missing her and not seeing our three grandchildren.

How can Spirit enter into this situation and heal it, heal our family, the old family dynamic that has been with us for generations? How could Spirit heal if I was still substituting? I was not substituting with drinking, spending, or other means like I would have twenty-one years ago, but there was still that need to be first; to demand attention; to keep creating. Alas it was only just that; substitution for being a bad mother.

There I said it. Yeah, I know, I did the best I could BUT it was not the best for her.

For now I will sit and feel the pain of missing her and our grandchildren. The pain of years lost. The pain of shame. I can "LET SPIRIT HAVE ME."

Spirit loves me deeply enough to let me know that no one can give me an answer. Not Deepak, not Bishop Jakes; no one. I had the answer all the time. Like Dorothy when she found herself in Oz, there is chaos and confusion when we are called to search more deeply, but there will always be others to help along the way.

I believe there is a sacred code to the universe, the I AM code; a loving code. When we are not in alignment with this code, we are NOT in balance.

Today, if you gave me the choice to be on *Oprah* and receive all that goes with it or the choice of this insight, I would value the insight more. It is the insight I will take to Spirit when I draw my last breath.

With deep gratitude to Oprah and a special thank-you to M for that phone call.

Within a month, the doorbell rang. It was two policemen. Our beloved Melanie had taken her life. I fell to my knees. "Dear God," I pray, "is this what forgiveness looks like?"

Yes, I hear in my ear. *You will understand later.*

"Is this my fault?" I ask.

No, is Spirit's reply. *This is one of the many reasons you could not go on Oprah. Your relationship in public would have hurt her and you would have blamed yourself.*

"God, help me off this floor. I understand. Going underground, I do not stand alone."

Here is a poem I wrote about ten years ago for my daughter.

Reflection of a Shadow Self
Have you ever seen yourself through someone else's eyes?
Have you ever felt their pain, felt it was disguised?
Have you ever understood, what was the real intent?
You hurt them with words, and deeds that were twisted, crossed and bent.
Have you ever seen the damage when the heart it does not speak?
The memories were lost, found later in a heap.
Have you ever tried to reach out, to someone that you bore?
Only to be silenced and left with nothing more.
Have you ever felt the pain that twist beneath your ribs
When you flesh and blood is crying
Unable to feel amends that you did?
Have you ever stopped and looked way deep within yourself?
The shadow has arisen
GOD I need your help.

A story, a Dance, the beginning of self-love

In 1999, John and I began taking ballroom dancing. In 2000, just before he started his UN missions around the world for the RCMP as a peacekeeper, we were at a castle-like hotel in Ottawa. We had been dancing now for over a year and it was time to display our talent. It was showcase time. A time where we watch others in their full glory and a time for us to have fun, show off, and show up for one another. John decided he did not want to go that day. He did not have to show up for anyone. Not a problem, I would go on my own with our instructor. John would join us for the dinner and dance afterwards.

Well, he showed up in a foul mood after the tables were cleared; dancing this night was not his gig. I remember standing up against the wall, looking at my tapping feet, feeling my beauty, and thinking, *I am too precious for this.* I wrapped my beautiful black gown around me, took off my silver shoes, and went into the freezing night to hail a cab home. I did not say goodbye or discuss with him where I was going.

I felt like Cinderella going home from the ball. If my knight was going to put up his armour or close off his heart, that was his issue, not mine.

I was content, felt gratitude, peaceful, and alive. I held no anger. I was with the Divine.

When I arrived home I went into the spare bedroom. An hour later a knock came at the bedroom door: "What happened to you?"

I was reading at the time and asked him to sit down. I explained how I felt. I told him that when he treats me with disrespect, when he chooses to dance the beat of the joyless knight, well it just was not my rhythm.

He went into our room and the next day humbled himself to say, "I am sorry."

We have been together since 1973; forty years, and I am happy to say that when the fairy wants to dance now, her knight is very accepting.

The hole in the floor

It had opened up again. The last time I'd seen that hole was in 1995.

Melanie had just left in chaos after visiting us, John and I were in a flux—I believe it had been days since we'd last spoken. I was saying the serenity prayer; a prayer that had been my mantra since 1991, but it was not working that day. I wanted something to soothe me. A drink was not the answer, I was afraid of the hangover. I was afraid of God's disapproval. (I do not believe in this disapproval as I write this.)

I was afraid for my life. My life was filled with light and shadow. I loved my job with Crabtree. My health was good and Amanda okay. Melanie was out of the house on her own with her children . All seemed balanced. But I did not feel balanced. I was not going to any doctor to be put on meds. I had my PRAYERS. They had been working for the last few years. *What the hell is wrong with me today? That hole keeps inviting me in.*

I was close to it on the floor and as I peered down I knew there was no turning back. I knew deep inside of me that there are a few who are now in institutions make that decision to leave their minds just before they enter the darkness and say goodbye. They do not say goodbye to their life but to life, as they know it. They want out, they want someone else to look after them, feed them, dress them. They are tired and just want to BE.

As I very slowly got closer and peered deeper into the hole, I was confronted.

Suddenly, jaggedly I was pulled and found myself on the other side of the room. I looked around but no one was there. *What the hell?*

My brain cleared, *Oh yes, hell, why go into it when I can live it right here?*

Ouch, that was close. Get dressed silly girl, get to work, cook dinner, go live your hell, don't tell anyone how you really feel but go find some other tools to try and understand yourself. Heaven is just around the corner.

Saboteur or Gambler? 2004

I was given one of the first offers that could have changed my life; I have had many in this lifetime, as I am sure most of us have. Sometimes these experiences can make us crazy; these decisions, these choice points. Those moments that can shift everything. When they are happening, we are not aware, not in tune, until days, weeks, or years later.

On this evening it was from Mr. Prana and the CEO of a well-known institution—from Australia. They were courting me as we sat in a small restaurant in Bali on the beach in Jimbaran bay this gem of a restaurant—nothing fancy; fresh fish, and salad. At this establishment you had the opportunity to pick your fish from one of many tanks and they fried it up for you.

The question these gentlemen, very gentle men, are asking: "Are you interested in teaching Reiki to our staff here in Bali?"

I would be provided for; food, accommodations. I would need about three months; I was told, to train everyone in their hospitality kingdom.

I declined. I was working for Crabtree & Evelyn and Scantrade and I had a deep sense of responsibility to these companies in Canada.

That evening I had forgotten my responsibility to self and what I really love; this love of teaching all that I have learnt thus far about Spirituality. That evening in March of 2004, I was feeling unusually calm, happy, and at peace. Why make changes to something that was already working? I was visiting Bali regularly; I had a great job as sales rep for marvellous companies in Canada. All seem logical. This would be a Gamble.

Note the word logical. "Common sense is not so common."

I was thinking with my head, not my heart.

That October I was back at CMED, studying with Caroline Myss. We were casting our wheel on Fate vs. Destiny. I asked her if could she give me insight as to why I was afraid to leave my job with Crabtree. Her response was direct and true. "Lilly, you are just scared of losing your stuff."

Ouch, she was right. I had to go home and rethink my life.

My Fate at that moment was living in comfort; my Destiny was to shift in this comfort. Get real.

Well now if that won't drive you bonkers, make your mind buzz, and your heart pound. Change, again? Shit. I thought I had done all that was required to change in 1991 when I entered a twelve-step program. This saga of changing myself, to become aware, to take a role in my life instead of just allowing it to unfold, makes me dizzy. It feels like spiritual madness. And yes, I am MAD I have more work to do. It requires work—hard inner work. It requires a mission statement, a printout for my soul.

It took me two more years to leave Crabtree. How would I survive without an income? I was always stealing from my future, constantly in debt.

Plus I loved travelling alone on my own across Ontario in that small 2002 Jetta.

If my life is working, why do I need to change? Is that what you are asking? Good question. I needed to enter that small still voice within and ask myself, "How do I best serve others and the planet?"

When I take my last breathe, am I going to tell myself that it was because I had comfort, and stuff, or was it that I did my best to serve others? Could I serve others while working the way I was? I said yes. I could still give my Angel workshops, still write my poems, and see clients for the Trinity Table. I could find the balance. As I write this, I now see the madness to that thinking. A few months later I realized I had to quit Crabtree, as I was not in balance. I was doing too many things. The customers at Crabtree were no longer a priority. I was getting paid a lot of money for doing nothing and my inner thief was not going to have any of that. It was okay to steal from myself but not others. I called my boss, Helen in June 2006, told her it was time for me to leave. She was very loving. She knew this was not an easy decision as she was aware I loved the product, the people, and the travelling.

The day I called her was the day I wrote my foreword for *Lilly White Lies and Dreams*, a book of poems. I was now free to only work on spirituality. We were told it is hard to make a living in this work, but that was not the reason I was so excited every time I gave a workshop, wrote a poem, or put someone on the Trinity Table. This work put fire in my belly, not food.

Bulgaria, Greece and Angels.

In 2005, Melanie invited us to visit her in Sofia, Bulgaria.

We arrived a few days before Easter—March, a cold dreary dark day. I was excited to see our daughter and her wee ones again, and the excitement continued as the plane landed. I thought the airport would be bigger, grander, but like everyone else we departed the plane on the runway and walked to the Arrivals.

Melanie was there with her driver, a bodyguard, and her male companion. She presented me with flowers, much to my surprise. We went outside into the night and were escorted to her car, a Bentley. Mitch, her husband at the time, was nowhere in sight. I was confused but asked no questions. Mitch's job was with communications there in Bulgaria and security was important. We arrived at her home and it was a Grand Hotel-like atmosphere. I saw her touches of Easter at the front door and was delighted with her creativity. The house was huge and her staff and her chef greeted us. *Where are we? Who is this child of ours?*

The next day I was treated to a spa treatment. After the treatment I went to the gym and met her trainer. I was well aware of who he was, as he had been her companion at the arrival gate last evening at the airport. Nice, good looking, and polite. Perfect guy for our daughter—the problem is that she is married to Mitch and as of yet we have not seen him. After our outing I arrived home and as we went up the elevator to the main dining room (yes, the house was so big, there was an elevator), I asked her where Mitch was.

"Oh, he is in the hospital with heart issues," she said nonchalantly.

I was shocked as we were in his house and everyone and everything seemed normal. *Jesus, he is ill and no one tells us about it unless we ask.*

He arrived home Easter Saturday. Sunday there is a wonder-filled Easter egg hunt for the girls and their friends. Melanie's companion is there and John and I are in a state of absurdity. It all appeared like such a farce and meaningless. All fluff, no substance. No one talked or said anything. We were to keep our mouths shut. Say no evil—for to me this is evil. I was horrified. The next day, Mitch left on business. That night Mel left the house after the girls were in bed and arrived back home in the wee hours. I awoke in the middle of the night and began packing.

John tried to calm me down. "We can't leave."

"Yes we can," I replied. "This is madness and I do not want to be around this"

The lies, the deception. This is our child and she is acting like a word I will not repeat .

John said,"Think about the grandchildren. Stay for them."

I settled down, unpacked my suitcase, and resolved to accept what I could not change. I slept a restless slumber and dreamed of dangers to come.

A few days later, after she became aware I was not a happy houseguest she suggested we go to Greece. It was only an hour flight. Just the three of us. I complied, hoping we could talk to her and resolve my fears and judgments.

We arrived in Delphi, one area of Greece I had not yet visited. I had been to Crete with Caroline Myss, in 2002 and John and I were in Santorini in 2003.

Delphi is known for its Goddess energy and I had been wanting to visit that place. Goddess is one archetype Melanie carried within her.

We settled in and went for a walk. She wanted to tell us something but was unable to. I had a feeling she was pregnant again but I never actually found out. She did not bring the child to term. Again I can only guess who the father was.

With Melanie, I had never been wrong. EVER. I knew my daughter. We were sitting on a hill overlooking the beauty of this sacred space. The grass was soggy and I put a sweater down for us to rest upon. John was getting us a soda, so she and I had a few moments together. I felt the Divine and peaceful energy enter us. She was picking at the ends of her gorgeous hair as she usually did when she was contemplative. I asked her if she was okay and suddenly I looked up in the sky and saw a cloud in the image of an angel. (This picture is on my first book of poetry, *Lilly White Lies and Dreams*.). I grabbed the camera and took pictures of the angel and Melanie. In that brief twinkling of time, I understood the significance of, "All is in Divine order, God is working on all your problems, stay out of the way."

I was stupefied into silence and I did not ask questions for the rest of our journey. I allowed the unfolding of Divine order.

As a mother I worried but I knew enough to Let go and Let God. My concern was my business, not hers. The rest of our journey to Delphi was filled with hope.

When we arrived home in Sofia, we spent another few days playing with the girls.

Before our departure to Canada we tried to speak to Mitch about a few concerns, but he did not hear us. Again I repeated to myself, *It is not our lives or our business.*

After our return to Canada, I did not hear from her until a few months later. She called and said she had breast cancer. I panicked and booked a trip to leave three days later to be with her in Sofia. When she found out I did this, she panicked and was very angry with me. She insisted I not fly to see her.

I realized something else was going on. Perhaps she was having breasts implants, as she did have them at one time and this was her way of telling me she is in the hospital. Another day of madness. But I loved her; this love she did not understand. Her dad had cancer at her age so of course I was concerned. Alas, I heeded her request and cancelled my flight. A few days later she let me know she was okay.

I tell these stories so you know what madness can look like. I was never sure who was in psychosis, Melanie or myself. What I saw drove me crazy. What I felt was numbness. It all seemed surreal. If I have any regrets today, it would be that I had known more about bipolar mental illness. Instead of feeling angry, making judgments, and detaching for my own sanity, I would have been more helpful. More of the Good Mother.

You may have a relative; a child; a friend who is acting out. His or her behaviour has you questioning everything, even your own sanity. These loved ones are not to be overlooked, mistreated, and labeled. They are ill and in need of help. Sometimes the help—the treatment works. For Melanie it was too late. But her death is not in vain. She is directing me to write about this illness. She is aware her children will read this and that now they will understand the authentic her. Not the actions of an outrageous woman.

Actually she was outrageous. Maybe that is what made her so special. She was a police officer, a fire fighter, a decorator, a real estate agent, and a business owner, but more than anything she was a loving mother to her three children. She left them but she also ensured they would be looked after through the men she loved. I always said that she was so bright; she blinded herself from her light.

What we lost in the fire

"I want my family back," she said, it was July 1st, 2010, and we were at the Esso station in Rexton, NB. She was purchasing a bottle of water. We had just spent the night with her and the grandchildren. Chaos was everywhere, but God how I loved her. When she looked at me and said those words, I was spellbound. That moment, that one moment, it changed everything; my cells, my DNA, my destiny. She wanted to be with us—that was all that mattered. "Sure," I replied. "Let me talk to your dad."

At the time, John and I were the happiest we had ever been. He had just returned from another UN mission. I was working and loving our life in Almonte.

In 2006, we had bought our dream home, our castle at 29 Christian Street, Almonte. I was hosting workshops, a friend of mine, Suzanne, was giving yoga classes. We were planning another Power Up Your Life weekend. All was good.

However, Melanie wanted her family back.

We went back to Ontario after our weekend in New Brunswick.

We sold our castle in three weeks.. The movers were due to arrive on our doorstep Sept 2rd.

On August 27th, a Friday afternoon, I was sitting at Groundz coffee shop in Almonte with a future employee Valerie. My cell phone rang—it was Melanie. "Mom, are you sitting down?"

"Yes, why?"

"The house you purchased from us here in New Brunswick…I am sorry to tell you, your house just burnt down."

"No Worries, Spirit has something else planned," I replied. But I was not so sure of anything. We had no home. *Shit, now what? What now?*

I actually lived out of a car for thirteen weeks. Stayed with friends, Amanda and hotels. I was free. I had my weight scales, blender for morning shakes and mirror. All set, letting spirit have me until a home was built.

Retail, not a fairy-tale

December 2010—I was in tears, talking to John on the phone. He was in Haiti on another mission. I had just moved into our new home with the help of good friends.

I wanted to open the White Lilly, a boutique for ECO-friendly fashions. John was doing a good job of convincing me I had truly lost my mind this time. (his intuition is very good and he was seeing our future) . I was known for taking risks; jumping off the cliff and landing on two feet with open heart, but this time around though, really? He reminded me that I was fifty-five years old. I told him I was not retiring down, I was refiring up. "How did this happen?" he asked.

Where did I lose it? Hm, let me take you back to see if we can find it together.

John and I were to have moved to New Brunswick on Sept 1st but as you remember our house that we were to purchase had a fire. We decided to stay in Ontario and as I mentioned earlier ,I literally lived out of our car. I stayed with friends and Amanda during the thirteen weeks that our home on Johanna St was being built.

In October of 2010 I had been with two friends in Bali on a yearly spiritual journey.

Michele, Louise, and I were in the city of Ubud the day before we were to return home to Canada. We were running to catch our driver when I stopped and stood motionless, There in front of me, GODDESS ON THE GO. "Hey, girls, there is my store."

"What are you talking about now, Fairy Lilly? Come on, we are going to be late." Once we were in the car: "Do tell."

I explained that on December 3, 2005 I was in Holt Renfrew looking for an outfit to travel in, which was trendy, fashionable, and hip. I had looked all over Ottawa and by 3:30 p.m. I was on the phone talking to my friend Cyrilla, complaining that I could not find anything, anywhere that was easy to care for and easy to wear.

Cyrilla's reply: "Bella, tomorrow you are leaving for Bali, make your own designs."

Duh, why didn't I think of that? You have to love friends who are your champions. When I arrived home that evening, I got on the phone and I gave her a few design ideas. I cannot draw so she sketched them for me, plus a few of her own ideas. She faxed them to me, and voila, I was on my way.

When I landed in Bali, I conveyed my idea to our good friend and spiritual family member, Agung Prana and asked if he could take me to some of the designers and manufacturers he knew. Agung Prana used to be in the garment industry and had many connections. I made contact with some of these manufactures but I was unable to articulate my designs to them. I was looking for a material that was washable and great for travelling. I envisioned jackets long and short; trousers; leggings; handbags; and body wear all colourful and complementing one another.

Timing is everything and this was not the time, so I tucked the designs away for future reference.

Back to 2010. The girls and I returned home and I immediately searched Goddess on the Go on the Internet. Voila, there they were, still under construction. I had an indisputable feeling about this company and I was ready to jump off an additional cliff. I made a deal with Spirit. *Okay Spirit of inspiration, here's the deal. I will take this next assignment on two conditions. If this is my next adventure, I will be able to rent the new space in Heritage court. If Gord Pike, the landlord of Heritage Court is at the location when I visit the space today, I will know it is gelling and the universe is in order and doing the work I need to proceed The other condition is that I have John's full support.*

Yes, Gord Pike is at the location in addition to his wife Bonnie.

I told them my plans and we made an agreement—an understanding of faith and belief in one another.

The store opened April 20th, 2011. It took a mere three months to get the premises ready. I hired the best in the business, Charlene, to help with the design of the store. Diana makes up my logo, and staff was hired. I returned to Bali in February to order and meet glamorous Janet O'Malley, designer, and entrepreneur extraordinaire. My first order was for $24,000.00. I purchased another line called Animale and silks scarfs galore.

I checked astrology chart and looked for a time to open this next journey. 1:00 p.m., April 30th. Most of the planets were in the ninth house. Opening the store with so many planets in this house meant that I no longer would focus on myself. The focus would be on my relationship with the world. How the store would govern itself I did not know. It was the planet of spirituality; long distance travel. We created an altar at the entrance so that all who entered were blessed. This was not only the business of selling, but the business of soul. Breathe life into it.

Shite, here we go again. I was open one month when Melanie called on my cell. "Mom, are you at the store?"

The most heart-wrenching decision I ever made

It was June 15th, 2011. The phone rang at the store.

"Mom, Belinda [Mel's fifteen daughter] is in the hospital with a suicide threat. They have her on the psych ward."

My first thought was, *Mel is going through what her dad and I experienced for years when she was a teenager.* History repeating itself.

But keep reading. The story gets interesting and doesn't have the outcome you think.

I had just opened the White Lilly the previous April, 2011 and on May 30th my mom and two sisters, Kathy and Deborah, had visited. One evening, the four of us, Mom and siblings, decided to take a look into our astrology charts. I do not consider myself an astrologer, but I have been studying the heavens since 1998. It was also very much needed for my work as an archetype consultant. After we looked through our transits, I decided to glance through Melanie's. Ouch—Pluto square Pluto. That can be a tough one. Pluto is about transformation, change, and maybe the death of something; a dream, work etc…I looked into Mel's daughter's charts. They both had Pluto aspects but not as severe. I simply looked at my family and said, "We might lose one of them. Let's hope this is only about another move or a deep change."

After the phone rang on June 15th, I packed up my bags and planned to fly east the next day. The staff would look after the store. This was serious and more imperative. It was also familiar to me as John and I had experienced this many times when Melanie was in her teens.

I received a few calls from Melanie all through the day, but they were not about her daughter. They were the strangest calls about her Botox appointments scheduled for the next day, asking if I would I go instead. I thought this request so out of place but not out of character for her. I said I'd talk to her when I arrived the next morning. Her phone calls became so persistent I stopped answering, even If I thought something had happened to our granddaughter. I would have to deal with it upon my arrival.

A friend of mine picked me up at the airport and dropped me off at Melanie's husband's work so Mel could pick me up there. It was close to the hospital. Upon Melanie's arrival I was stunned to find her spaced-out on drugs. I was horrified to see that she had our other granddaughter Maddie in the car with her in her state of slurred speech and tipsy walking.

We got in the car and instead of driving to the hospital she said she had one stop first.

While we were walking up the steps, my granddaughter informed me that this was where Mom got her face done. *Shit! Damn! I have been hijacked yet again.* Being bested by Melanie was common.

Upon our entering, the doctor took me in her room and as she began to speak about my face I stopped her. "Look at me, look at this face, I really am okay with how I look today and with who I am. The issue here is my daughter. I realize you are treating her on a regular basis and for the love of all that is holy, SHE IS ONLY thirty-six years old! Why are you giving her this? Do you not realize she is an addict?"

The doctor apologized and said yes, Mel was in her office regularly but after talking to me she would monitor her more.

We had begun to leave the office when Mel said, "Mom, you have to pay for your treatment."

"I did not get one Melanie. I am beautiful just the way I am."

Now don't get me wrong. At fifty-six years old I would have loved a treatment but my granddaughter was present and this was for her ears. (She still remembers this and brings it up regularly.)

Now back to the real story—our other granddaughter wanting to die.

We finally got to the hospital and I was allowed to spend the afternoon with my beloved fairy. She had made many friends and we had a wonder-filled afternoon.

I returned the next day, took her out to her high school graduation and observed ONE thing only.

The next day I told the doctors and nurses, "YOU HAVE THE WRONG KID IN HERE."

She was trying to get the attention of her mother. It was her mom who needed to be there.

In the evening I received a call from Social Services. Was I willing to speak to them about Melanie?

"Yes," I replied. "But it will not be easy."

John at this time was on a UN mission in Haiti. We spoke for hours that evening on the phone, as I was so confused about meeting with Services the following day. If I told them the truth about Melanie, they might take her children, but if I did not, the children might die. It was Melanie or her kids.

The pain of this choice drove me into convulsions of fear.

After our long talk, John wrote her a loving letter; a letter about her taking responsibly for herself and her children; a letter about her growing up and stopping blaming others, and a few more words of love. John is a man of few words so this was an exercise of expansion for him.

I cried myself into a restless sleep. Nicole my girlfriend who I was staying with made my coffee the next morning with words of support to send me to the gallows. (That is what it felt like.)

At the hospital a lovely women and I met. There were many questions and I did not lie or hide anything. We spoke of what I'd witnessed and what I knew, plus Mel's behaviours since she was a young child. The sadness was overwhelming as I loved Melanie and my grands equally, but I felt like I was betraying my daughter. I am sure a mother's betrayal must be the worst sin of all. Or is the sin of seeing your grands in danger the foulest? We had done everything for Melanie up to this point; I needed to save the kids.

The heaviness, oh the heavy sense of fate versus our destiny.

I spent another few days in the area, visiting the hospital, and taking the other grandchildren out for dinner. Finally the evening arrived for my flight. Nicole my girlfriend was driving me. We stopped in to say goodbye to everyone at Mel's home. Her last words to me were: " I know you called Social Services on me. You call yourself a mother."

These were the last words I ever heard from her. Almost a year to the day later, Melanie was dead.

The nurse called me. "I am sorry we did not listen to you and bring her in."

"Thank you" ,"why is everyone afraid to discuss mental illness," I asked. Be aware, Never afraid..

I only tell you this story not to make it look like Melanie was a bad person. She was not well. She was brilliant and beautiful, but something in her brain was not congruent. She had a mental disorder.

You need to take a look at your life. What are your behaviours that are not consistent with health, love, joy, compassion, and hope?

What in the name of all that is holy were you thinking?

JOHN was right.

That is the question I ask myself today.

I was running a store, taking appointments for White Light (the Trinity Table,) giving angel readings, playing fairy to grandchild, travelling to Bali and healing my grief. When anyone asked if I was I okay, it was: "Of course. Why wouldn't I be?" I was involved with this and that in the town of Almonte, always trying to stay on top of things. I had to know what was going on. My brain was full, my belly empty, my soul tired.

I awoke in January 2014 with a voice in my head: *Time to close the store, or it will close you down.*

Usually I do not fear this voice, but this day in January, I was frozen. I mentioned to John I needed to shut down by March. His reply, "Do you think you should close this fast?"

I said, "I opened in three months, I will close in three months."

Sure I knew people would talk: "What? She was only open for three years." But I did not care. When was the last time someone, anyone, lived my life?

March 15th arrived faster than a blossom in spring. I decided I was going out with a party; the same excitement and party as I'd had when we opened. Those who loved me and loved the store, they were the support. My landlord, who has since become a good friend, was very empathetic. Our accountant was behind us a hundred percent. Diana and Maureen ,my staff were true Goddesses filled with grace.

I opened the White Lilly because the timing was right. I had discovered Goddess on the Go, the eco-friendly clothing line, on an October trip to Bali. Heritage court was just opening in Almonte. At the time there was no other clothing store in town. Timing was everything. Not long afterwards other stores opened and I became very competitive. This is something I do not like in myself and after Melanie's death, I was not in the store much and made many mistakes. One thing I know to be true. No one will ever take this away from me. I actually opened the White Lilly for two people I came to love dearly.

One was a woman by the name of Dana. Dana would come in daily, walk around, stay, chat, and leave. She was about seventy-two, a loner. We were always polite to her and allowed her to stay as long as she needed. We would chat and she'd be off. When she found out we were closing, she came to visit me one day. She was in tears. "What am I going to do now," she asked.

I did not understand, so I asked, "What do you mean?"

She replied, "Your store is one of the reasons I get up each day. I have somewhere to go. You and your staff are always polite and you let me stay for as long as I need."

I was shocked, I had no idea.

We had an altar in the store, and I liked to believe that lighting a candle and spraying holy water made a difference to the energy. I had not realized how much.

The other reason I opened the store was for a young man of about forty. who has autism. You will see him walking around Almonte each day; rain, sun or snow. Each day he would come into the store to say hi and get his chocolate. I always kept candy on the counter for clients but in our last year of business it was always for him. When I was away, I would ask the staff to make sure there was something on the counter for our 3:00 p.m. visitor. When he found out I was closing he came in one day and sat on a chair next to the counter, and we chatted for the longest time. I came to find out he was brilliant. He loved to bowl and was more aware of everything around him than I had given him credit for. He was a true jewel.

The day I take my last breath, I will have no regrets about the store. It has put us backwards in debt, but the abundance I received can never be calculated. Knowing these two people has enriched my life beyond my humanness, but my soul knows.

So many of us carry emotional scars and baggage from our human experiences.

We can lose jobs, homes, bank accounts, a child, a family member, a friend, or a relationship.

During these times of loss we feel like we are losing our minds; our footing. We do not have tools to walk through our sorrow. We think, *I'll be okay, this pain will pass.* I call this pain, "The Awe of the Raw."

I now realize that the anger I felt when we lost home, daughter, mother, and business in a three-year period was not anger. It was the Pain of the Raw. Of being vulnerable, exposed.

I lost all of these in three short years with the exception of my marriage of forty years. During that time, John's and my union was in question but we worked through our dark night with a few tools. We had to reconnect with our core selves first, and then with each other.

During a recent trip to Bali, a good friend said, "Lilly, you have not allowed your sorrow to come through."

I recognized that grief was about me, my ego. Sorrow was about sadness. Not the raw of the pain but a deep, deep sorrow. I decided to enter this sorrow much like you would go into a well.

I entered this well much like I would enter my sacred space in our home. With respect and curiosity.

When I returned from the well I realized I had developed a few steps to help you and myself.

"Power Up Your Life," through grief of any kind.

1. Respect Your Sadness: Take some time to enter into your heart and feel the sadness. Allow the tears to flow, quietly, peacefully.

2. Let Go & Surrender: Letting go of an energy that you trust in is a wonderful way to allow your ego to get out of the way. That energy you may choose to call God, Higher Power, higher self or someone who is carrying you; an angel, a departed love one. Light a candle to this energy, breathe in Love as you light, and breathe out Hope.

3. Nurture yourself: Look forward to your favourite cup of tea, a daily walk, and a prayer you repeat each day. (This can be a song.) Remember your true essence. Go back to when you were very young and embrace that wee one, reintroduce yourselves to one another. Take time to play. Eat wholesome food. Yes, chocolate and a good glass of wine once in a while will not hurt you unless sugar is an addiction. If it is, nurture yourself into letting go and find something else that you enjoy. Almonds, hummus, and peanut butter shakes have always helped me. I am an addict so sugar and wine are out for me.

4. Know thyself: Listen to Caroline Myss, author of *Sacred Contracts* and her series on archetypes. Once you know yourself you are much better equipped to witness thyself.

5. Create: Whether it is the life you want, or perhaps a painting you have been longing to create. A book you have been meaning to write. A cake

you wanted to bake. You get the idea. Get your creative juices flowing. Start creating new memories.

6. Embody the whole of the holy: Sit and meditate daily. Five minutes or an hour. There are no rules. Allow yourself to just BE.

Say a mantra such as, "I choose to be awake in my life, participate in my being, contribute to my community, allow joy to have me."

7. Let Spirit have you: Just for today, one day at a time, allow yourself the freedom to step out of the way and "let spirit have you." You can awake each day with the question, "What is my assignment today?" Allow the day to unfold with YOU as a participant, doing your daily chores, rituals, and responsibilities, but witness what is showing up for you.

8. Read Anne DeBurtt, *The Grief Abyss*.

Whatever your pain, my hope for you is that you believe in yourself enough to light the power fuse in you that only you can ignite.

The Code of Silence

A **code of silence** is a condition in effect when a person opts to withhold what is believed to be vital or important information voluntarily or involuntarily.

The code of silence is usually either kept because of threat of force, or danger to oneself, or being branded as a traitor or an outcast within the unit organization. (Wikipedia)

A code of silence can be an illness onto itself. In this story it is within the family dynamics—of course I am going to be judged, criticized.

On one of my trips to Calgary to see Mom before her departure, I wrote one of my many poems. It was July 2013.

Damaged

Can you not see the damage you've done?
Six little kids
Always on the run

We ran from your rage, your anger, your fear
You beat us dry till there were
No more tears

It was confusing and crazy
You never let up
Said we were lazy
We were quick to shut up

We are all adults now
Five of us still stand
Now we realize
You were the child
But never the man

I sent this to one of my siblings.

"Oh dear, you better keep that under wraps," was the response.

At this age we are all adults. Fear and anger follow us to our graves if we do not work through it. They boil inside us like a pustule and pop open and ooze all over someone when you and they least expect it. Even in this anger there is a code of silence. No one wants to talk about it.

Usually it's called "being sensitive." Frequently Mom would say. "Your dad and I are fine when we are alone but as soon as one of you kids are around there is always a fight. You Hancocks are all so sensitive."

No, Mom, we are all mentally ill in one way or another. Either we are addicts, or ego busters, bullies, or tormenters. Or, in my case, all of the above.

When one sibling calls you a crazy bitch, and another a fudged-up fairy, there are two things you know for sure. You have touched a wound and words have power. They can tear down a building; someone's self worth. Words can destroy generations of healing. If that is not a sign of illness, I do not know what is.

When a major family member dies, when there has been no resolution within the family, when there has been no ownership for actions—nothing changes. Family members will go to the next in line and take all their anger and energy out on that person. We are not brave enough to go within and change ourselves. That would be taking responsibility for our words and actions. It is easier to blame. The madness coagulates. It can come in the form of our eating habits, our daily routines, our waking moments, our moments in darkness. Food can be one reason for our madness. Yes it's also an addiction but few of us understand the results of eating what is not good for our bodies or our DNA.

I firmly believe that if Melanie had monitored her intake of foods she would be alive today. She was like her sister to some degree. Celiac runs in our family.

Melanie was lactose intolerant since she was a baby and whenever she ate sugar she was turned on, turned up, turned inside out. Her behaviours were monitored and we witnessed change as soon as she ate food. She thought we were crazy and would not listen to our advice. A year before she died she began to drink alcohol. Our family's worst enemy.

We were inherited addicts from generations ago. I was in process to stop the disease in our family, but it was clear it would take more time than I thought.

It was no coincidence that Melanie took her life the same week my mother was diagnosed with stage-four colon cancer. Neither of them ever paid too much attention to what they ate unless it was to diet.

We eat to nourish our bodies; to have healthy mind, body and spirit. How we feed this miracle of who we are is evident in the results of our daily lives. How do we feel when we wake up? How do we feel at 3:00 p.m. in our day? How does that first drink feel?

How do our bodies respond to what we put in our mouths? How do our brains react? I will not go into all the details here. You can research plenty on the Internet these days.

What is this Love we all talk about?

We feel it, we breathe it, we live it. There will be no right or wrong answers. We all have our interpretations based on our experiences from the moment we decided to enter our mothers' wombs.

The balance of love/hate, addiction/sobriety, obsession/acceptance, withdrawing/reacting can play havoc on any relationship. We need to sober up for ourselves and understand that once we recognize and study the medical applications of addiction we can make decisions.

With addictions in our family, the important lesson I absorbed was that love does not have to be a combat.

Cruelty

I wonder if people really know what cruelty is. Some think it is physical abuse, or emotional abuse only. Cruelty is much more.

It can be shutting down in silence because we are afraid to express our feelings because we have no idea what intimacy is.

We may be in our forties, fifties, and sixties and not be motivated to change because we are lazy and have no desire to find tools for living. We shut everyone out, protecting ourselves and not realizing the viciousness. We are not aware how it cuts the heart, the soul of another. We have no idea how this gets passed down through the generations; how it becomes a part of the collective, the planet, and the universe. The whole New Age concept of, "I cannot be around that person, it hurts me," has gone to extremes. Everything in moderation. Self-help has gone to me, me, me. Where is the "thee" in me?

I know someone who is out there talking about his accomplishments, trying to inspire others to reach their potential. I have a saying, "You can climb every mountain in the world and until you forgive, you will never reach your highest peak." This person has no use for his family. At a funeral he thought we were vultures. He is unaware that it was he who wanted and wanted, not us. We were getting rid of stuff. At another funeral in 2000, he totally took and took. He controlled the whole estate, not once asking his family what we wanted. We forgave him—we loved him anyway. He continued to ignore his father, his siblings, and the cruelty of his actions did not dawn on him. He had no idea and that is cruelty of the worst kind.

"The inability to know thyself." Not being able to walk your talk. To forgive and love unconditionally is the only way to release, love, and let go.

To love others as they are is the paramount gift we give this planet and the contribution we leave our children's children.

To be vindictive, spiteful, and unforgiving is not being inspiriting. It is being cruel. It is a form of madness that gets passed down through generations.

My father hated his father all his life. He passed this animosity down to his children and we have had to work very hard to walk into the future with love. His reason for this hatred began when he was eighteen months old. His mother, Lillian died at twenty-six from TB. Dad was adopted by his aunt and uncle. Dad never forgave his father for what he said was, "giving him away." Grandfather Hancock had four children. His decisions are not to be judged, Stan , my grandfather had his own stories. Cruelty seemed to run in the Hancock family. Spitefulness for something we are powerless over can dip slowly from one generation to the next. It seeps in the bloodstream of each new creation and cannot, or will not, drain unless we are aware and brave enough to make the changes.

The madness of lies, whys & ties

Lies are very deceptive, (now there is a truth).

There are white lies we tell so others will feel good. "Do you like my hair?" she asks.

"Why yes," I reply. (My thought is, *No, I do not like the color. You look ten years older.*) Usually when I am this blunt and I have been, I am told I am arrogant, bossy, cruel…So most days of late I just keep my mouth shut, and nod my approval from my head not my heart. A chakra bypass.

In all of my fifty-nine years. I have never said anything to anyone intentionally meaning to hurt or cause pain, except for Mothers Day 2014. I myself was in deep pain and when someone called me a crazy bitch and chaos freak, I went into that crazy bitch. I intentionally said words to hurt. (I was on line with two people at the time.) I wanted them to feel pain. I was fed up with holding my feelings in for fear of hurting them, especially in the last three years. You might call that May 14th a breakdown between my head, my heart, and my throat chakra.

There are lies we tell to protect others from pain. Yes, it is a form of control and not allowing the other to feel the "awe of the raw." We sometimes think we know better. That is usually a lie also. We do not know better. That is the Ego having its way. God/ Goddess is love; thoughts are our will, our ego.

There is the lie of protecting ourselves. In previous chapters you have read about my lying as a child when I was in trouble and afraid of the consequences. One day I told Dad I had actually done something when I hadn't. He (as usual) found out and questioned me as to why I would say I had done that thing and taken the penalty when in fact I had not. I remember looking into his beautiful blue eyes. It was him with the tears this time and I said, "I don't know."

But that was a lie also. I did know. I knew I just did not care any more. I was damned if I did and doomed if I didn't.

For many years I have been more truthful than I should have been. I tell everything, I lay it out for all to see so that nothing is hidden. The issue with that is we are all mirroring each other. When someone sees the truth about themselves through my words, deeds, or actions it may be too difficult for them to see. They then go to the number one lie: gossip. God, I hate gossip. It steals the very soul of who we are, who we are becoming. The thief steals from the one gossiping and the one being gossiped about.

We all have our interpretations, perceptions. How you see, hear, and feel is going to be singular to you.

Then there is the denial lie. The disowning of ourselves and being unable to see what is in front of us.

What is most accepted? The sneaky lie or the lie of denial? You know that lie when you feel superior…that the person in front of you needs to change? Everything is their fault. They are the damaged one, the crazy person. You go about your life and are with your family but never take ownership of anything. You find it impossible to go deep inside and dig around. You say things like, "Move on, the past is past," but you still stay the same.

In my humble opinion, this is the worst lie of all. I know someone who is angry all the time. She calls everyone a liar. She will tell you her interpretation of something that happened with no regard for your views or your perception. She is always right. If you disagree, you are losing your mind—get out of her way, she just might kick your heart out with her spiky heels.

The lie of silence.

Once upon a time not so long ago, there was someone in my life who I thought was honest. She would not steal anything material from you but she could steal your energy. She had low self-esteem so every time she spoke it was, "Should I do this? Does this look good on me? What do you think about this?" On and on it went. I loved her. If I'd known then what

I know about her today, I would have called her on it. In her words I was a bully, a sorceress, and more words of abuse not worth mentioning here. I now understand that when I spoke to her, asked her questions, she never understood what I was saying. She saw and took my words upside down or backwards. (After much research I now am aware of her condition.) She is unable to hear what is being said. If she had opened up to me during those years instead of keeping her anger and silence and talking about it to others who passed on the information, we would have been able to work things out. On a cold Thursday morning in February, she attacked me with her angry voice in the most damaging way. This person who studies spirituality and prayers, is always in a workshop of some kind, the, "I do no harm to others," let me have it with both barrels. When she was having her meltdown I was silent. I wanted to say three things. I did not, she was already in pain, why cause more?

1. Yes, hit me at my weakest, I am losing the store, my child and mother have died in a year, my father has had a stroke. Yes, beat me when I am most vulnerable, you coward, you.
2. Oh my God, you are acting out just as Melanie did. I guess I have killed our relationship just as I killed Melanie. (That lie I have dealt with. I did not know I felt that way until that moment. That is why she is a noble friend. Put here by spirit for a good reason other than what I thought.)
3. This all sounds familiar: "Isn't this the reason you left your spiritual family a few years ago?

Worst of all, I lied to myself on how I saw her, knew her. I loved her false self, her mask. Now that I have seen her, I still love her. More now because I really SEE her as she is. She has been a noble friend. I have emailed her, birthday, condolences, etc., but she will never forgive me.

Most New Age followers these days have a slogan: "I need to detach from those that do not understand me." I need to leave Kevin because he does not see me." I call this watery spirituality; swimming in your lies. Skipping over the work that needs to be done. Not being brave enough to enter the shadow. Trust me, this women is getting advice from someone who thinks they know but has never allowed themselves to enter both light and shadow. Very few of us have such courage. Perhaps courage comes from being beaten for eighteen years, who knows.

Allowing, "Spirit to have us," is, WHOLE, WHOLLY, HOLY. Not just part time.

In her mind I am to blame. Yes, I am to blame for many things in that relationship. I own my part. I do not lie about that. Hopefully before she takes her last breath she will understand that she was loved. I hope she comes to understand that if you are unable to forgive, you have not helped transform this planet. The real reason we are here.

Then there is the lie that tricks you. It is the lie of believing we cannot make a difference; that we are too small in such a big world. We need to dissolve that lie and get out there to make a difference if only for the smallest of reasons. Enjoying a good cup of tea with gratitude or running the tea company. Do it with the belief that you are no small, body of love. You belong here on the planet just as everyone else does.

Be big to thyself.

Love is an action word

Did I love my parents? Of course I did. Did I like their actions? NO. You cannot say to live one way and then act to the opposite. This was confusing to me. Yes, I understand addiction and madness, but we all have choices. What is more important, that liquid you drink, your mate who is disturbed by the drinking? The debt for the dress, the cigarette we smoke or the one we claim to love? I have in the past few years fallen in love with my father. I have forgiven. I see him as a child in pain and I relate to him in that child archetype. Now we play together when we chat on phone or when I am blessed to visit him every three months in Didsbury , Alberta where he is living out his final days.

I have a passion for cloves cigarettes. I did not discover them until my first trip to Bali in 2003 when a friend offered me one. "Oh, I do not smoke," was my reply.

"Try this," she coaxed.

I did, I was hooked. There is very little nicotine in these wee gems and they are filtered with sugar. I love them. They are my peace pipe. I smoke only when in Bali and upon my return to Canada I let them go. I am finished with them until my return to Blissful Bali. However, upon our arrival on one of our Florida trips to Flagler I found a tobacco shop that sells something similar. They are called small cigars as they are imported from Indonesia and would not sell if labeled cigarettes. I purchased two packs and began the next morning while having my morning cuppa and watching the waves on the Atlantic ocean. Peace, tranquility, and memories of Goddess Melanting (a Balinese Goddess) wash over me as the smoke cloaks my outside surrounding. Heaven is just a drag away. John accepts my obsession but is not happy. One Sunday morning after our return I had one and became nauseated. *Strange,* I thought.

Later in the day I tried another and was immediately sick and went to bed. I thought I was coming down with something.

Monday morning I jumped out of bed as I smelled John's delicious brew and went outside to light up my day. I could not stand the smell or the taste.

I went inside and asked John if he had prayed while at church the day before that I would stop smoking. His look, that sheepish downward dog look, said yes and he gazed up and echoed, "Yes, why?"

"I cannot smoke any more." Later that day I tried again and as I lit up I realized that if John disliked my smoking that much, if he was that worried about my health, then I had a choice. Him or the smokes. I chose him. I do not miss them. Actually every time I think of them, my stomach churns. His prayer worked or maybe my love for him is action not words.

How often throughout our day do we give thanks?

Count our blessings and talk to God/Goddess? If you do not like the word God try, "Good Orderly Direction." Sacred can be minuscule throughout our day. It can be watching a bird, putting our back up against a tree, staring up at the moon. For some, it can be private moments with another. It may be going to church and being with the Divine in a sanctified space. My travels to Bali opened my eyes to prayer and sacredness. From the time the Balinese open their eyes they are in gratitude and prayer. There are altars in their homes, yards, rice fields, streets, communities, towns, and cities. They have altars in their hearts, they alter their consciousness. They go to temple regularly with offerings to their Gods. They take offerings out on the street, in their cars, and on their motorcycles. Sacredness is everywhere.

As I write this, I now realize why my home and yard is filled with altars. In the morning I light three candles; one for the planet and one for my family, which includes siblings, spiritual family, and friends. I light one for the health of my mind, body, spirit and the health of my relationship with John. I had an altar in the store I opened in 2011, "The White Lilly." Each morning we lit a candle and sprayed holy water, which I would bring back from Bali. The magic was that when people entered they stayed and some would comment that there was a certain energy in the space. I would grin and thank them, but I knew it was the spirit of love that was in the store.

Blood, Stress and Fears

I was at the final day. I was manic. In all of my fifty-nine years I have not been manic. The good news: I was NOT bi-polar. The bad news: I was trying to come off this god-forsaken drug. The doctor had given it to me when I had shingles for the second time in six months. I had lost a child, my mother was dying, my father had a stroke, and I was losing my business. The doctor said, "If you cannot look after yourself, I will." So I took it—the shingles were driving me crazy.

After a few months, I was home and the store was closed. Yes, I was dealing with the watery grave (another chapter on debt), but I wanted off this drug before I left for Bali October 25, 2014. That is where the real healing is, Beloved Bali. I go through hell, but that's okay, all is in Divine Order.

For some crazy, unknown reason I cancelled Bali. Then I was slam-dunked into the abyss. I was through the hole in the floor, the crazies. This day, we learned our beloved granddaughter had two cysts on her brain. Well that I could not handle. I called Ellen, a friend I met while studying at CMED. "What do I do to stay sane?" I asked.

"Just be there for them," she replied. I needed to hear her voice.

Martie in Lilydale, said, "You are the Ninja grandma." That I could envision. I could be strong, at least for Amanda and my grandchildren, if nothing else. I decided to count all the things I was grateful for. It started with calling those I trust to be in prayer so healing could begin.

It had begun, the miracle of prayer. The unity in community, to nourish mind, body, and spirit. Yes! They called next day and the cysts were benign. She was going to be okay. Nothing to worry about. But it was the sweat, the stress, the fear. What are we really made of? Can we keep going when difficult times are upon us? "Yes," I hear a whisper in my ear. "When you can't, others will. You only need to trust that and believe."

For the love of food and our addictions

My good friend Kerry Ford has written this piece and I thought it a valid piece of information for many of us with gluten intolerance, or celiac disease. Our love of food is or can be another addiction and loving ourselves enough to monitor ourselves and what we put in our bodies is another form of self care. Thank you Kerry. You can find out more about Kerry's work here. http://www.panandpanacea.com

If you love your body and your brain, pay attention to this chapter. We are what we eat.

What is gluten?

We throw the word around so often these days that we've almost become intolerant to the word itself. Because gluten issues are so common now, we also have no actual idea of what gluten actually IS, except that it lurks amongst our favourite foods and denies us our deepest joys —a baguette slathered in butter, mom's lasagne, that muffin with our morning coffee... So let's get clear on what we are actually reacting to here.

Gluten refers to the proteins found in wheat endosperm (a type of tissue produced in seeds that's ground to make flour). Gluten plays two roles—it nourishes plant embryos during germination and also affects the elasticity of dough, making your coveted wheat products chewy and irresistibly easy to sink your teeth into.

Gluten is composed of two different proteins: gliadin (a prolamin protein) and glutenin (a glutelin protein).

Gluten both nourishes plant embryos during germination and later affects the elasticity of dough, which in turn affects the chewiness of baked wheat products.

Gluten is actually composed of two different proteins: gliadin (a prolamin protein) and glutenin (a glutelin protein). Gluten is made up of these two major proteins, gliadins and glutenins. But twelve minor components make up gliadin and a person can be sensitive to one or more of all these components.

(GS) (Gluten Sensitivity) is an exaggerated immune response to gluten. Inflammatory messengers form, which migrate to other parts of the body, including the brain. GS condition can lead to celiac disease, a serious, life-long autoimmune condition with damage to the small intestine. GS, on the other hand, can occur without any gut involvement. But in many cases leaky gut results and other food sensitivities can occur. Leaky gut is a condition where the gut lining becomes weakened because of gluten and other factors, and larger food particles can pass through, causing immune issues.

Modern grain vs. ancient grain

This is a super important distinction.

Modern foods contain up to forty times more gluten than traditional grains, and modern gluten can be addictive. (GS) Gluten sensitivity seems to arise mainly from ingestion of gliadins in hybrid wheat and deaminated wheat. Deamination is a process used in modern bread making that makes wheat more water-soluble.

The brain drain

Gluten can also pass through the brain blood barrier. Research links GS to schizophrenia, epilepsy, depression, bipolar disorder, autism, ADHD (attention deficit hyperactivity disorder), migraines, and other problems. Perlmutter describes several of his patients with ADHD who improved significantly through a gluten-free diet,

When gluten gets into the blood stream, it binds to the brain's morphine receptors, which creates a mildly euphoric condition and a reward effect.

Nutrients

Perlmutter describes several of his patients with ADHD who improved significantly through a gluten-free diet, and with the addition of probiotics, resveratrol, vitamin D and DHA (docosahexaenoic acid). However he misses the boat when not including vitamins A and K2 as part of the package when recommending vitamin D because all three are needed together. Fermented cod liver oil is a natural source of all three vitamins—A, D, and K2.

The probiotic + Caesarean link to gluten sensitivities

Research shows that babies born through Caesarean section have a higher risk of developing ADHD because they miss out on the probiotic inoculation that babies normally receive when passing through the birth canal. Breastfeeding is also important in that it may dampen later immune response to gluten and the development of food sensitivities.

In the past, laboratory testing existed only to diagnose celiac disease, and indicators for gluten antibodies were not positive until a certain degree of damage was done. Thus celiac disease is referred to as a "silent disease." Today, testing through Cyrex Laboratories has been developed to identify GS in its early stages. Because research shows that mothers who were gluten-sensitive are fifty percent more likely to give birth to a child who later develops schizophrenia, it is important to identify and control gluten sensitivity early on with a gluten-free diet, especially before pregnancy and childbirth.

The consciousness piece.

Something is asleep in us.

It is now being unveiled by the study of epigenetics, a branch of modern medicine that understands a new layer of energy and genetic expression of the foods we ingest and how they can both alter and suppress our own Divine genetic expression.

Likewise, ingesting highly functional, non-hybridized, non-genetically modified, ancient forms of food that are standing in THEIR own genetic expression, can awaken us to our fullest potential for thriving longevity and wholeness as a species.

Remember that we pass these genetics on to our offspring. And just as is true in the study of neuroplastics (the ability to alter our brains), our genetics are now known to also be mutable, changeable, and pulled out from underneath of a mass veil of unconsciousness, damaged from modern-day processed diets.

Our pliability as a species – in other words, our adaptability – is our lifeline. Adaptability is what keeps species alive and thriving for centuries. We are facing an environmental crisis like we have never seen before and our ability to survive and subsist off of non-foods and genetically mutated versions of what our bodies can recognize, is being tested to its fullest extent.

Our food is consciousness itself...It either awakens us or puts us to sleep. Makes us alert and intuitive, instinctive and alive, or is slowly killing us. Inspires creativity, co-creativity, a sense of community from inside to out, or it shuts off our deep, human instinctual desires for connectivity to life, community, family, and creativity.

Ancient grain vs. modern grains

If you have issues with Gluten, which most people do nowadays, one simple tweak may show significant benefits. However, it is important to note that all aspects of health must be addressed to truly eradicate the core issue and to re-establish a strong gut ecology and healthy gut lining.

Einkorn

Commonly known as einkorn, *Triticum monococcum* is an intriguing heritage grain that was harvested as early as 16,000 BCE. Cultivation began during the Neolithic Era and early Bronze Age (10,000-4,000 BCE) and continued into the early twentieth century, when much of einkorn production was replaced by hybridized, high-yield, pest-resistant strains of what we now recognize as modern wheat—created for modern agricultural purposes.

As mentioned, einkorn is not the same as modern forms of wheat. When einkorn is milled into flour, you will notice that the grains are much smaller than grains of modern forms of wheat. Moreover, einkorn grain does not have the crease that is present on the side of modern wheat grains. The reason why the grains are different is the fact that humans have slowly and steadily altered wheat genetics by choosing seeds that delivered more gluten and promised higher yields, as they were ideal for large scale production and distribution in larger farms. As for gluten, einkorn has a different kind of gluten compared with modern wheat because it does not contain the D genome, only the A genome. This is significant because the most popular test for detecting the presence of gluten is based on the presence of the D genome. Although Einkorn does contain gluten, it's a different type of gluten, and will not fail an Elisa test.

Einkorn is nutritionally superior to hard red wheat, supplying higher levels of protein, fat, phosphorous, potassium, pyridoxine, and beta-carotene. It's also much lower in problematic gluten. Enthusiasts of einkorn believe it tastes better, lending a "light rich taste, which left common bread wheat products tasteless and insipid by comparison," according to the ASHS publication *Progress in New Crops*. What's really garnering attention, however, is that einkorn may be nontoxic to individuals suffering from gluten intolerance.

Protocol and pantry overhaul

If you have serious gluten issues, I recommend a protocol designed by a licenced practitioner capable of guiding you through a detox AND rebuilding phase of your issues. Because gluten destroys the cilia in the intestinal tract and has a damaging effect on the gut, there is a serious rebuilding process required to create a hospitable environment for thriving health.

1. **Wheat Free does not mean Gluten Free**
2. **Gluten Free does not mean Healthy**
3. **Follow an anti-Inflammatory Diet native to your heritage.**
4. **Follow a Body Ecology Diet rich in fermented foods. (Importance of Probiotics)**
5. **5. Quality Over All Else**

RESOURCES
1. **Grain Brain**
Grain Brain. The Surprising Truth About Wheat, Carbs and Sugar, Your Brain's Silent Killers by David Perlmutter, MD, with Kristin Loberg. Little, Brown & Company. 2013
http://www.westonaprice.org/book-reviews/grain-brain/

The Heartbeat of A Marriage 2015

On Sunday, Oct 4th, John and I touched a millstone of forty-one years married. I was seventeen when I met him, I will be sixty soon. We have been together double my lifetime.

He was away with his twin brother last weekend at a hockey tournament. It was not necessary for me to party with him. We have had many days of sunshine, joy, and bliss over the years. This year, however, was different.

My parents used to ask me when he was away, "Lilly, don't you ever get lonely?"

"No," was my reply. I have no reference point for that. I am never alone; the spirit of love, bonding, and God is with me daily.

"Makes no sense to us," they would say.

On the last weekend leading up to our anniversary, reality peeped in. I began to feel the disconnection and allowed myself to surrender to that force. I realized that love is a force of energy that weaves its way in and out of our being. I did not feel empty. If anything I was full. I knew we had been blessed to have the years we'd had. They were not easy years. We went through John's cancer and moving twelve times in twenty-five years. My addiction, Melanie's bipolar illness and eventually her death. The death of a business and other deaths in our family.

We also had many wonderful years.

The births of our two children, our five grandchildren.

John's work, his promotions.

My creativity and absolute joy to live each day, one day at a time.

My success, my failures.

Our abundance, our debts.

We had lived in balance. We lived in the light and the shadow of who we are, either when alone or together as a unit.

What a road our lives took us down. We took that journey together fearlessly. When I told a friend we were thinking it was time to separate, she said, "Yes, usually when a couple loses a child the promise is broken. The death of a child can be, though not always be the death of a marriage."

"Yes. I said. "I am aware of that but I was sure we had suffered enough and we would not be a statistic."

Still, I was okay. I believed that whatever spirit had in store for us, based on the decisions we had made and the decisions we were to make, we would be just fine.

I went about the business of living. I watched our grandchildren. I rested, I wrote. I went to the gym, all the while knowing we were where we needed to be.

Was I scared? Yes, I was about to jump off another cliff. This time he would not be there to catch me.

I was going to be alone with the spirit of ME.

Then, the most magical day happened in the midst of the grandchildren visiting. We all had our wings on, and John was playing with us, serving us our dinner at our make-believe restaurant. Our two granddaughters both looked up at him as he brought us our drinks and as I looked at the girls I saw how they felt about him through their eyes. That look of trust and love— their giggles and yells as they said, "Yummy. Thank you Monka." Their name for John. Yes, thank you John, your trust and love, your loyalty, your passion, your acceptance, your ever-desire to change. To change for no one but you. That sexy ability to let go, forgive, and move on. Yes, I am blessed and stay together we will. It's been a busy forty years together. Maybe now we can slow down and let spirit have us.

Living together in healthy harmony takes more than a family. It begins there but it takes a community living in unity to nourish our Mind, Body, and Spirit.

We need to talk about what we are experiencing and do something about it. Not from our victim, but in the archetype of a warrior. To stand tall, find our path, and push through whatever we do, to live in our healthy environment. No one is going to live our mission but us and we must be committed to change.

I know we traveled the distance for one another. We were passionate, chaotic, neurotic but above all else lovable. When I take my last breath I want to see John's face or know he is waiting for me through the veil.

"Ya, Just for today I am going to let the spirit of John and our Marriage

Isn't life grand?

You see, all the gloom in *Madness, Addiction & Love* has a Beautiful, Blissful, and Bright conclusion. The chapter on love is how to get out of the darkness and onto living your highest potential. You now have the tools to "Power Up Your Life."

I was blessed to trademark "Power Up Your Life, tools for intuitive living" after I spent a weekend with Andrew Harvey. It has taken me twenty-five years to develop these tools, live them, and pass them on. When I am writing, teaching, and lecturing, I know I have been into the darkness. I have come out on the other side stronger. It is, in my humble opinion, the effective way to teach. I did not follow anyone else's work besides Caroline Myss's. & Andrew Harvey . I wanted to have my own experiences, not something out of a book that showed us how. My hope is that you also allow your self to feel the Awe of the Raw, take these tools, and love, and live them.

I am excited to know that most of us understand the Collective. When Caroline Myss called me the day our child was being buried, she mentioned the Collective. She said that I was not alone. Someone else is feeling and holding my pain. I could let go. I immediately felt release and folded into acceptance of what we were about to do; say goodbye to our baby girl—the mother of our three grandchildren. Grandchildren who are braver than anyone else I know. The courage they showed that day and which they continue to grow into, gives me great hope for the future.

I love knowing and feeling that when I am in shadow, someone else is holding my Joy. When I am in Joy, there is someone out there holding the shadow. When someone is in Joy, I celebrate them.

When they are in pain, I light a candle on one of my many altars.

All in Balance. We are not alone. The collective I AM THAT, YOU ARE THAT, and MORE.

Love

My hope for you is that you take from this book the belief that we are all mad in some sane way. That is our right to be human. We are all addicts if you look deep enough. It might be a small addiction to shoes, control, work, or power. It does not need be a substance.

And lastly, I will talk to you about collective LOVE. The true reason you are on this journey.

We can take drugs, blame our parents, go to war, be in and out of institutions, or blame God but mental illness is never going to subside in our society until we understand why we are here. What is our highest potential, our mission? Where do we start to learn this? Start teaching the "spirit of our tomorrows," to our children and their children. Teach them that indeed they are enough. The smile on their faces each day will move the stars in alignment—it will move the tanks out of the way—it will move the God in them to be better co creators with the universe.

Love is not physical; it is not about needs being met. It's loving ourselves with our flaws, defects, courage, strength, and so much more. It is about healing the inside as well as the outside. The mind, body, and spirit. It is being healthy enough that we attract a healthy mate. It is only in this way that we confront and comfort each other's needs instead of demanding they be met. Love is not a personal need; it is meeting each other personally in a loving embrace.

Madness and Addiction can be healed, controlled with medication, support groups, and acceptance, but my belief is that more than any of these is Love. You can see as many doctors as you need, you can take as many drugs as you desire, but unless you are in love with self and a power greater than you, it is impossible to feel love from others. Once you commit to yourself and your esteem with the power of spirit only then can true healing begin.

I have added a few comments from friends who encouraged me through the writing of this book. I asked a question one evening on Facebook as to what they think Love is. Here are a few insights.

Howie Kerr: Love is hope, hope and trust that the gift of love that you offer to someone is held as precious as you would hold a baby bird.

Heather J Hay Charron: Love is an integral part of my sacred contract "to do no harm." As I fulfill my purpose in this life I become more and more drawn to this expression of being. As I write this, Lilly, I become filled with the peace that passes all understanding. As a child I remember hearing the pastor say that benediction, and I wanted to feel it, even once. How blessed I am to feel it daily now.

Bonnie Giles: Unconditional acceptance and respect are the cornerstones of Love

Craig Morton: Love is knowing what you know and seeing what you see. You still not only want but need her, so that your life is complete and fulfilled.

Robin M Singleton: Love is unconditional. It survives through good and bad. It cries, but survives. It allows space, but survives. It knows when to walk away in sorrow, but survives. It doesn't die in spite of no longer liking. But there are times when you are forced to close the door on it in order to survive. Love and hate are two emotions that are incredibly close and when pushed too far by either one, the other, in pain, will take over.

Deborah Owen Sohocki: Love is keeping my heart open to others, myself, and LIFE no matter the temptation to shutter and close my heart. Love is courage to keep walking the path of life with an open heart to ALL experiences, people, the planet, and the universe.

Julie Huot Baker: I know you're TOTALLY not talking to me Lilly... but what's love as I know it today? To see you in all your glorious "flaws" and embracing it ALL as beautiful and critical to my understanding of who I am BECAUSE of knowing you...Love pushes us as much as it cushions us.

SEAN FURLONG, What is Love?
Love is what we spend our life trying to find

It is that moment that stops time. When everything is experienced from a different realm. Our senses are heightened our heart beats quicker and our longing is for that moment to last forever. Well it does.

Once we have experienced love we never forget. Any of our senses bring immediate floods of memories and feeling back as real as the day we first experienced love.

Human's life long emotion is to experience love. Love of another human being completed us and allows us to focus on other ways.

Just as our spirit longs for love our souls longs for love too. The divine love we need our soul to embrace. The support and friendship of good souls we meet whom we call friends. They are in some ways extension our ourselves and brings us together by divine intervention

Once we are content in love we see the beauty in our surroundings. The warm breeze on a summer night, the smell of earth and flowers after a rain, the warm glow in our gut from a beautiful song, the flavour of a drop of wine upon our tongue. Can it ever be any better than when we experience and appreciate these moments in our existence?

This is love to me.

Despair - have you ever been in des-pair?

Personally, I have never experienced the depth of despair. But that doesn't mean I haven't had a cause. As I sit on the shores of Bali, I think about the word despair, and I realize the significance of such a beautiful word. After all it is only a word...Despair—beauty in pairing of light and shadow. It is the word pairing. It is the balance of light and shadow. Most of us will only go into the shadow. When we are brave enough and courageous enough to witness both, we will choose light. Instead of despair, we are only in dis-repair—in need of repair. Repair is a form of healing and there are many tools to choose from. It may be the tool of physical healing, emotional healing or spiritual healing.

On December 1, 2014, I boarded a flight to blissful Bali. I had been feeling splintered and in need of repair. My ego thought it was only from a spiritual aspect, but in reality, I was about to embark on a journey of the trinity three: "mind, body, and spirit." I arrived in Bali with food poisoning, water retention (I looked like a puffer fish), and anger. For twenty-four hours I struggled with physical healing. I spent four blissful days at Puri Taman Sari. I experienced a channelling session with a priest and his wife Ade and helped release the pain of my mother's separation from the earth. I released my ego's attachment to her, released her soul to the cosmic stars where she is shining in unison with her ancestors, her beloved son Derek, and her grandchild Melanie, our daughter.

I experienced giving reiki and healing to a guest at Puri who was comatose. Within fifteen minutes she was up and walking. I experienced seeing orbs in my room and fairies galore. It was indeed a day of spiritual healing. I proceeded to go into Ubud where I meditated and prayed and had a day of play. Before midnight, my body was pushed into a hole. Spirit was saying, "Now it is time to work on your body. You are not listening and this is our way of speaking to you. In the last six years you have lost focus and it is now time to go into the body and listen."

Sometimes when we are so numb we cannot hear. Spirit will speak to us through a person, a place, or a thing.

Agung Prana, a dear friend, said, "Ibu Lilly , (Ibu is Mother in Balinese) ,there is so much darkness around you." I asked him what that meant in Balinese culture. His reply, "You have lost your way."

Well shite! I thought I had been following where spirit was directing.

It then occurred to me, when I opened the White Lilly, a boutique to help women feel good inside and out, I began to follow another path. I wasn't paying attention to my physical healing abilities and got caught in competition, ego, and death. In Ubud, Indonesia, falling into the rabbit hole was Spirit's way of saying, "You are not listening—now we have your attention. Your attention had been on experiencing happy and your sorrow has been stuck in your joints and in need of repair."

Okay, what now? A trip to Jatiluwih with Ibu Lynn and Mangku Made is needed. Okay, I am in the flow. My ego doesn't want to go and I am thinking Ginger, the cat, is helping me to heal. When I am with Mangku Made, he is very clear that when I fell in the hole, my soul stayed there. Now I need to call my soul back.

I have been very, very tired and for those of you reading this who know astrology, I have Pluto square Saturn and I am experiencing an internal death and transformation anyway. I am thinking that my soul in the hole is a far-fetched idea. But I trust Mangku Made and am open to his suggestion of a crossroads soul retrieval.

Well, the shite hit the fan. I had no energy. All I wanted to do was sleep. It took two days of nothing but rest and filling my body with nourishment. On the third day, I rose. Finally.

When we are so tired that we can't see into the next hour, it is the soul's way of being completely naked. It is the soul's way of screaming Eckhart Tolle's words of "be here now." My choices are few so I surrender.

In that surrender, there is peace, joy, and strength. Upon awakening on the third day, the fairy is back. Despair was not necessary—I was in need of repair.

What do a few pages on despair have to do with the chapter in this book on love?

When we let spirit have us, when we are in the orgasmic dance of love and spirit, the universe will bring us people, places, and things to help heal us. In this scenario, it was people. When people love us unconditionally, they contribute to our healing. They love us without considering our defects of character; they only see our energy and aura. These people who come into our lives, they love without judgments and we realize we are mirroring each other. A true healer is not textbook savvy but is one who heals through the power of their suffering. That is why they know what is needed and that is why we trust.

Trust is love. It is a collective unison of giving and receiving without question. In trusting, we are telling the God-source and the universe: I LOVE YOU. It was never about despair. It was about repair and letting spirit have you.

Silence is golden and you are worth your right to that gold. For love

What is silence to most of us? Peace, tranquility, calm, quiet?
It is interesting how we demand silence, crave silence, need silence.

When we truly go into silence the miraculous happens. Extraordinary, phenomenal happenings appear everywhere; in us, around us. While in Bali last month, John and I took a group of eight to this magical island with an unusual portal to the unknown. For me to begin to explain the wonder and gifts of this trip you will have to read another time. Today I would like to discuss silence.

John and a few of the others left to return home to Canada on the eighteenth. Two other goddesses from Alberta stayed with me until the twenty-ninth of November. We prayed and played together daily with each other and our spiritual families.

One day we decided we ought to have a day of silence. At least for a few hours. We voted on the next day and would start with six hours. The night before, we informed the staff at Amertha Villas where we were staying in Pemuteran of our plans.

The next morning we awoke. I went on my own to the ocean, the Bali Sea, at around 6:10 a.m. and sat with my pen in hand. A staff member bowed to me in reverence and brought my coffee without having to say a word. They did the same thing with our lunch.

Within a half hour, the girls joined me for breakfast without a whisper, only an undertone of love and respect. Once finished we went our separate ways for a little while and later joined once again to sit under a tree on the Bali Sea. No words were needed. The silence was soft, easygoing, forgiving.

We wrote, meditated, and walked slowly when we were up and about. We breathed deep into the heart of who we were and into the delights of who we are becoming. We prayed with love for others and we smiled inwardly with gratitude.

I had the most unique experience with our daughter, Melanie. I began to write to her and she wrote back through me. You may read it in my Wordpress. Lillywhite.wordpress.com

It is called. "Oh Melanie, Oh Mom. Messages from my daughter"

In this silence, food tastes different, air is soft, sky is brighter, smells are deeper, and everything is AWAKE because we are still.

It is a humbling experience and I recommend a few hours of silence weekly, monthly, or whenever you can. Do not sabotage yourselves with maybe or might.

Give yourself an hour at first, perhaps three. Let others know you are not available for those moments. A few days after I returned I gave myself twelve hours of silence. John understood. The people you love will understand. You are not running, you are praying and playing with the Divine in you. Yes, I realize you have children, jobs, commitments. But really, how good are you at this if you never take time for yourself?

Silence is golden and you are worth your right to that Gold.

A state of homelessness

Around and around we go.
Ultimately, I stop and this is what I know.
In my youth and numerous years later, I was spinning.
Why do we have to be in our twilight years before we stop?
Because the ego is tired?
Maybe we have studied ourselves to a point that we stop trying to be anyone else but who we are.

I don't know about you but when I was young, it was all about me.

Yes, grant it, I was always doing, giving, but my memories are of energy spinning around ME. There is a fine line between being unique unto ourselves, and being a part of a collective and understanding we are part of the whole.

Most of us spend our time wondering, worrying about ourselves. It's laughable really. As I told my daughter so many years ago, "We only have on average, seventeen seconds to impress someone. They are more worried about what you think of them." So what is this thing, this energy in us that needs to be validated, loved, and accepted.

Feeding our egos. Maybe most of you reading this cannot relate. Some of you can.

There is a state of homelessness in our environment and the ego suffers.

A state of homelessness.

Not having a safe space.

It does not matter who we live with, what level our education is, or our income.

When we lack self worth, self-esteem, we are afraid of being humiliated. When we are feeling humiliated it is difficult to be at home in ourselves. We continue to lose our inner power and energy. Our light becomes dim.

When we walk into a room, we either do not want the attention or we demand it. Living for others and what they think can turn into madness. If we are looking for attention, that can become an addiction.

As we age, as we go deeper into the soul of who we are, we come to an understanding— none of it matters. Matter is no-thing. Energy is every-thing.

We can learn to be at home in our bliss, our contentment, and our peace.

The next generation?

I like to think they are much more evolved.

They will pick up the torch, light the home fires and shed more light where it is needed.

Once the state of homelessness is healed in ourselves, then we are equipped to be of service to those who are truly homeless. Those who are living in destitution. There are plenty living on the streets we can now give our attention to. Finding a safe space for others, that would be a sacred contract worth living for.

Dying to be awake, Madness & Joy.

In 2005 I took another group to Bali on one of our Blissful Bali spiritual Journeys. This trip was different right from the start. My husband John was coming with me, as well as our daughter Amanda and her fiancé Mark. Family, support. Yippee! This trip would be filled with enlightenment for all.

It started off well enough. Picked up at the airport by our spiritual family, Agung Prana and his son Wah. We settled in nicely without incident. There were after all fifteen of us and we had just flown for twenty-four hours. We settled into our private villas, swam in our private pools, ate and had a starry dreams night. Next day we left for Taman Sari, one of my favourite places on the planet. North Bali. Coral reefs, fresh Bali food, full moon, Balinese dancers. In the morning, yoga on the beach, fresh fruit for breakfast, Bali coffee and then a two-hour workshop on my work, *Manifesting the Magic in You.* Based on Caroline Myss's work, the archetypes.

Later, the afternoons were filled with open spiritual discussions, swimming in the Bali Sea, massage or meditation. In the evenings, we enjoyed fresh fish, fresh fruit, and many more Balinese dishes made for our delight. Then it was off to temple for holy prayers. Beautiful colors, children playing, praying, baskets of offerings to the gods. There was so much to see, feel, and embrace.

After a few days we were on our way to Agung Prana's home in Mengwi. We were invited to stay at his home, which houses many villas, and a restaurant. Orchids everywhere you go. Lilies the size of dinner plates and butterflies surrounded us in vivid colors. It was with wonder that we watched the family and staff going about their lives in joy and bliss. There is no word in Bali for artist, as everything they do is with reverence and creativity. All is sacred.

One evening we all decided to have a channelling session. A priest, and Mrs. Prana's sister were our channellers and we sat in silence in the family temple. After a few minutes of prayers, the channeller began to make noises and scared a few of the group. Some approached the channeller, sat with her, and received messages from their relatives who had passed on. One young women's mother came to her and wondered what she was dong in Bali…The channeller then began to sing to the young women in English, a lullaby that the women's mother had sung to her when she was a child. The channeller did not speak English so we knew this was the real deal. The group was transfixed. I went to sit down next to a priest and immediately went into a trance. I went under as some would say. I fell to the ground—fainted is how my family described it. I remember feeling heavy and leaving my body, looking down at everyone but laughing inside. I then saw the panic on their faces. My husband John and daughter were not amused as they told me later they and everyone thought I was dead I was so stiff with hardly any pulse. Upon awaking with many blessings and holy water from the priest I awoke with the greatest of JOY I had ever felt up to that time in my life. It was pure, sacred, holy, and whole.. I stared to laugh. I laughed at the way we as humans think, act, talk, and behave. I laughed at the way we take ourselves so seriously. I began to witness everyone, everything in Technicolor. The world goes on, we leave at some point and we and everyone around us is saddened but there is nothing to be sad about. It is truly all holographic. All is happening at once. Nothing is what is seems. I laughed for days after my first experience in 2005 and have been privileged to experience this time after time when I am in stillness, in meditation, in Bali or here in Almonte on the Trinity Table. Once you experience the power of this joy, this bliss, you are forever changed.

You can access this experience anytime. Some of us only need a few tools. After the suicide of our daughter, I went into months of turmoil. I was able to witness myself in grief, the anger, the denial, and finally the acceptance. BUT I have had many days of JOY and BLISS. The Power of allowing Spirit to have us is indeed empowering. There will be days that spirit will guide us to allow the shadow to arise, to experience any grief we are in or the loss of anything in our lives. Or, we can experience the Joy, the Bliss of the Divine. We will find the laughter, the funny bone in us any time we choose. Yes, it is that simple and you do not have to go to Bali. You can if you want. I often have a trips planned and the next one in Nov 2017 with Andrew Harvey.

Come experience for yourself the Power of Joy and Bliss. The POWER OF YOU. POWER UP YOUR LIFE. Start laughing for the innocence, the joy of our lives. Start dying to be awake. Experiencing death is when we are fully awake.

Evolve; get involved with your health

While with a client I was amazed with her story as to why she was sitting in front of me. Her story could have been taken out of my own personal journals from the eighties.

She was ill, that was easy to see, but not the waiting for a hospital bed kind of illness. This was, "I feel nuts. The doctors cannot find anything wrong with me." They finally gave her meds for her itchiness and said she has fibromyalgia. She had been experiencing panic attacks, chronic fatigue, sleepless nights; the list was long and very familiar. I realized at that moment we were mutating…our cells were changing. I asked about her liver. She did not drink, but she did say a test showed something abnormal on her liver.

In the late eighties while living in New Brunswick, I also experienced all these symptoms and was sent to doctor after doctor. Only when I entered a twelve-step program and stopped running, did sanity return. It was not until 1998 when I visited my naturopath doctor that I realized I was filled with candida. I started a long program of nine months to rid myself of this yeast that was attacking my cells.

As I listened, I began to realize that so many of us have experienced these strange symptoms at some point in our evolution. We truly are evolving into a higher consciousness and in order to have the eyes to see, the ears to hear, and the skin to feel this transformation, we must transform. We must allow our bodies to go through the mutation. The panic attacks for me were the ego not wanting to cross over into the unknown; the unseen that we all have access to. We are currently in the IN between. My body in here but I can at any time access the other world. My EGO shouts NOOOO! Panic…this is all subconscious of course until we awake.

Until we connect all the dots of who we are. Tools are readily available, be it through the lens of Symbolic sight, the Archetypes, Reiki, Angels, Body Talk, or Trinity Table, just to name a few.

Make no mistake we are all EVOLVING, now get INVOLVED, first with your health, your wealth, your family, and your community…

Into the depths of my being,
I awoke seeing, the possibilities laid before us this beautiful day.

Suddenly, I was filled with fear
At someone's else's despair
Her belief that she is not enough.

Her confusion of being
Has limited love's space to dwell where it's not safe.
The shame of truly showing one's face,
To stand up and say I am filled with grace,
Into this community I rise up and take my place.

A place filled with wonder, joy, and play.

Living today there is a new way
Of shining her light.
She is part of one community,
Her duty,
To be conscious of those around, to look with gratitude, joy, sharing, passion,
She is a Beacon of light, Bright in Unity.

St. Dymphna,

Did you know that there is a saint we can pray for mental illness and anxiety? I had never heard of her until I was in Flagler Beach, Florida. I had gone to church one Sunday morning with friends, Rose, Gloria, Sherry, Christine, and Wendy. The parish has a small bookstore that sells books, prayer beads, and statues. As I entered I felt a heat run through my body. I walked over to a table and there in front of me was a statue of a woman I had never seen before. I ask the clerk, "Who is this?"

"Oh that is St. Dymphna, patron saint of mental illness or nervous disorders."

I was stunned as I had just been thinking of our daughter on our way to church and brought money so I could light another candle for her as well as for my brother. I fell in love with St. Dymphna. I purchased her likeness and she now has her own sacred space on my altar. I pray to her whenever I am anxious or when I am praying for someone else who is disturbed. She is a gift of courage, love, and acceptance. Here is a little of her story taken from Wiki.

Her prayer is:

Good Saint Dymphna, great wonder-worker in every affliction of mind and body, I humbly implore your powerful intercession with Jesus through Mary, the Health of the Sick, in my present need. (Mention it.) Saint Dymphna, martyr of purity, patroness of those who suffer with nervous and mental afflictions, beloved child of Jesus and Mary, pray to them for me and obtain my request. (Pray one Our Father, one Hail Mary and one Glory Be.)

Saint Dymphna, Virgin and Martyr, pray for us.

According to tradition, as with another great saint, <u>St. Philomena</u>, St. Dymphna was martyred as a teenager for her purity when she resisted the advances of a powerful figure.

In St. Philomena's case, it was the Roman emperor Diocletian in the fourth century. In St. Dymphna's case it was an Irish pagan king named Damon, *her own father*, in the seventh.

Apparently, St. Dymphna's mother, who was quite beautiful, died when the child was only about fourteen. This so distressed King Damon that he sought to have his own daughter, who was Christian, take her place. (Talk about someone with a mental disorder!) Before this occurred, St. Dymphna had taken a vow of chastity, consecrating her virginity to Christ.

St. Dymphna then fled Ireland with Saint Gerebernus, her confessor, along with two others to escape the king. They landed in Belgium where they settled in the town of Gheel, but the king caught up with them. Damon then killed Saint Gerebernus and St. Dymphna as well, when she refused to return to Ireland with him.

As with St. Philomena's story, this account is given to us from tradition and its authenticity has been disputed, but the relics of both saints have been very powerful indeed!

St. Dymphna's relics were placed in a church built in her honour in Gheel, where she was martyred, and miraculous cures of mental disorders took place there in the centuries after her death. The town itself became a model of humane treatment for the mentally ill.

In the thirteenth century, the Bishop of Cambray commissioned an account of St. Dymphna's life's story based on the oral tradition and the miracles attributed to her afterwards.

An infirmary to treat the mentally ill was built in Gheel, also in the thirteenth century, and the town still cares for them to this day. Miraculous cures of mental illness and epilepsy as well, still occur at her shrine.

Prayers to St. Dymphna like the one above show her to be a great help not just to the mentally ill, but indeed, to anyone experiencing anxieties in these troubled times! Her feast day is May 15th. (Wiki)

You Are An Empowered Being Of Light

Now go set the world around and in you on fire. I have added this "30 days to Power Up Your Life" as a gift to you. If you are experiencing Madness or Addiction and are unable to find love, use these tools. I hope that you find yourself and continue to live in love.

POWER UP YOUR LIFE
30-Day Challenge
Workbook
By Lilly White
The Power Up Your Life 30-Day Challenge
30 Ways to Power Up Your Life!

Dear Reader,

In October of 2014, I had come full circle with my grief, sorrow, madness, addictions, acceptance, and joy.

It had not been an easy transition.

In three years we lost a home to fire, a child through suicide, my mother passed with

Cancer (she was diagnosed the same week our daughter died), Dad had a stroke, I lost

A business, and we lost our financial freedom.

Before I opened my business we had been debt free. This business had my heart.

The White Lilly had a spirit all her own. My archetype of fashionetta was thrilled to experience the birth of the store.

It was interesting to watch how my financial statements went into the red within a month

after our daughter's passing. When we are in energy debt we are in

financial debt as well; you cannot separate the two. I was in debt mentally, physically, and

emotionally for three years. I was in pain. This pain was misunderstood by many as anger.

I was living the awe of the raw. I say awe because living daily in such pain while visualizing love and joy in the days to come was an inspiration to me.

Sometimes I drank, sometime I did not. When the awe of the raw was so painful, my heart would throb and alcohol was the only antidote. I could feel my mother around in those days, we'd drink together, the insanity of it all. When I finally told John, I knew I had to start my program all over again; one day at a time.

I am free once again, just for today.

One brisk morning in February of 2015, while watching a robin look for its nourishment,

I pondered what had helped me through those dark, cold days between May of 2012

and October of 2014—days of feeling empty, undernourished, frozen. I sat down and

compiled a list that turned into the Power Up Your Life 30-Day Challenge. My wish for

you is that you take these simple tools and apply them to your everyday life when you are

struggling with something or have entered a dark night of the soul.

May you have fairy dust at your feet, laughter in your belly and joy in your heart, no

matter the depth of your struggle. Finding peace in our chaos—that is our Holy Grail.

Lilly White
Almonte, Ontario

The Challenge

In these next thirty days you will work with your mind, body and spirit. You have an opportunity to become happy, healthy, and holy (whole).

Let's begin your first ten days, one day at a time, one step at a time, to a new you — ten days working with your mind.

Ten Days Working with Your Mind

Day 1

A Day of Preparation

Let's get you ready to pray and play. This is a day of H.O.P.E.—Helping Others

Pray/Play Everyway.

Prepare an altar in your environment, either indoors or outside. An altar alters our

consciousness. (A voice from the unknown whispered this in my ear in 2003 while

I meditated on the shores of Bali.)

The energy of our altar uplifts us to a higher frequency.

Place something that is important to you in this sacred space. It can be a picture of

yourself or of someone you are praying for. Burn an incense stick; the burning brings

in the essence of spirit. Perhaps placing crystals, rocks or something you value at your

altar will help ground you today.

I like to have angel cards or archetype cards next to my altar. I pick a card each day

and allow spirit to speak to me through the card. I also light a candle, or two or three,

depending on what I am experiencing and who is asking for prayers.

"Invoking the Seven Directions" is a lovely way to start your day. I first heard of this from Joan Borysenko. Over the years I have revised it to make it my own. It only takes a few minutes, and the energy of love and trust lasts all day:

Facing the sun to the east with arms held high, invoke the angel Uriel. The light of God is the light of clarity. He beams light onto any person, place or situation. Uriel also shines light into any situation you need to heal.

Turn around to face west, and with arms held high, attune to the angelic being Raphael, the healer of mind, body and spirit. As you feel this healing energy seep through your cells, your memories and the spirit of who you are, recognize that you are in a moment of wellness.

Gratitude flows through your crown, into your body and down to your feet into the core of the universe. From this core you feel your body take in the iron of the planet, which is so important to your health.

Breathe.

Facing south, with arms held high, sing the praises of angel Gabriel. He shows us the strength in ourselves and others. "Gabriel, I choose to be alert. Thank you for sending me messages through a person, a place, or a situation. I am a witness to my life. I am learning to live with my life with non-judgment." The strength of Gabriel cloaks you with the knowledge that you are compassionate about yourself and the well-being of others.

With reverence, face north by turning around, arms held high. You are filled with joy at the presence of angel Michael; he who is most like God. In this moment you are filled with the strength and wisdom of all that is. This strength empowers you to live a courageous life; a life of passion.

With your arms held to the heavens, say, "AS ABOVE," and with arms to the

MADNESS, ADDICTION & LOVE

ground, say, "SO BELOW."

With your arms wrapped around yourself, say, "I AM THAT I AM."

You are a joy to the universe—to the God of your understanding—simply because YOU exist.

Angelic beings are aspects of us, of the divine source of the universe that flows through each of us. As a Catholic I identify with angels. I felt their energy as a child, and witness miracles through them. I also pray to Hindu devas, goddesses, Greek gods, Allah (the supreme

being) and Buddha (spiritual enlightenment). What is your belief is your truth. Own it.

Day 2

A Day of Inspiration

Take this day to read an inspirational book. To save time, listen to it while driving or

doing chores. Your library should have lots of inspirational books on CD, or you can

download audio versions from the Internet.

I love Anne Lamott's *Grace (Eventually): Thoughts on Faith*. It's funny, and a

quick read. Each chapter is a short story.

You will also enjoy these favourites of mine:

Kathie Donovan's *Inspiration in Action: A Woman's Guide to Happiness*

Jill Angelo's *Sacred Space: Turning Your Home into a Sanctuary*

Ellen Gunter and Ted Carter's *Earth Calling: A Climate Change Handbook for the 21st Century*.

Caroline Myss's *Entering the Castle: Finding the Inner Path to God and Your Soul's Purpose* and *Defying Gravity: Healing beyond the Bounds of Reason*.

Reading inspires us to reach further. Words empower our imaginations. We can release

grief when we read about someone else's experiences and realize that we are not alone. Words hold power. They cast spells and create magic. Stories take us to other worlds deep within and beyond our personal sacred space. We are a collective force, united on this planet in ways we are only now discovering.

Day 3

A Day of Writing

Buy a notebook or download an app from Apple called Day One (a simple, elegant
journal for your iPhone, iPad, or computer).

Find an hour either in the morning (sunrise) or evening (sunset) and go somewhere
to be alone—a park, the beach, a wooded area, your altar space, your bedroom —
somewhere sacred to you. Take your journal with you.

Sit. Relax. Breathe. Close your eyes. Go inside and feel.

What are you feeling? Write down that feeling—that one word that best describes it.

Look around. What are you seeing? Close your eyes again for a few minutes, and upon
opening them write down the combination of what you feel and what you see. What do you smell? Do not analyze this. Write down what you feel and see, and the smell or fragrance you experience.

Close your eyes. What sounds captivate you? Write down one sentence that describes
what you feel, see, smell, and hear.

You can now begin to write a paragraph about your experience. Try not to complicate
or overanalyze this experience.

Close your journal. Walk or drive home slowly, in reverence. Reopen your journal
another day. You will realize you were in the experience, in the frequency of God. If you
do not have a belief in God/Goddess, use G.O.D.—Good Orderly Direction.

Day 4

A Day of Listening

Witness how you react to something negative that someone might say today. It might

be a coworker, a friend, your spouse, a child, your parent. Pay attention. Are you listening? Are you hurting from what they are saying? Are you taking it personally?

Are you open to criticism? Are you quick to respond without thinking? Listening is not only about letting go and surrendering; it is also about accepting. If you hear a truth, own it. If this truth is not yours, there is no need to make a point or defend yourself. Listen, let go, and forgive. I have opened my mouth too many times because I was not listening. I may have been vulnerable at the time and took things personally, and my mouth went on a tour of "Yeah buts," "If only," and "You don't understand." I lashed out and caused pain. But when we listen with our hearts we can drink from the cup, the Holy Grail.

Day 5

A Childish Day

If you are blessed to have a small child in your life, play this day. Observe what this

wee one can teach you about the laws of the universe. Their inner universe reflects the

outer. "I am hungry." They do not have a time for hunger or need to think of hunger; their bodies tell them. "I am tired."

There are no rules except the ones we give them. They play, run, cry laugh, and nap spontaneously. They allow the spirit of who they are to have them.

If you do not have a child to play with this day, remember a day before you were seven

years old. Pick any day you remember laughing. Stay with that child for a few hours. See and feel where that child takes you. It might be the beginning of a journey into self-discovery.

Day 6

A Day of Silence

I realize that for those of you working at home with small children, with family visiting,

or with a career outside the home, this will be a challenging day. Welcome it. Awake with the intent to feel the stillness inside you this day. Have the intent to speak only when spoken to and always with kindness.

When you have intent and are able to witness or observe yourself, you recognize your stillness, your inner silence. Remember the song "Silence is Golden" by The Four Seasons: "Silence is golden, but my eyes still see."

Watch, observe, witness.

Day 7

A Day of De-cluttering

Junk stored in our minds is reflected in our surroundings. What old thoughts, old

memories, old wounds are cluttering up your freedom? Write down a list of five thoughts about yourself that you think daily. Try to think about ones that you may not be consciously aware of. For example, "I do not like my hair," "I need to lose a few pounds," "I eat too much chocolate," "I dislike confrontations."

Place your list of negative thoughts in a small dish in which you can burn it. Place the

dish on your altar, light it, and let it smolder. When finished, replace these five thoughts with five positive thoughts about yourself. Place these on your altar, light a candle

beside them, and bless them. The blessing can be "Here I am, Spirit. I see and feel

the beauty, the goodness in myself. I am a reflection of you and all that is whole. I am

letting Spirit have me this day."

Remove five items from your closet or bureau that you have not worn in the last year

— a pair of shoes, a scarf, a dress you have been waiting to wear when you lose those extra pounds. Give them away. Now, isn't that freeing?

Remove five items that have been sitting on your bathroom shelf getting stale and

throw them away. They are only taking up space on the shelf the same way your harmful old memories are taking up space in your mind. You might find more than five, so let them all go.

Go to where you store things for another day—the maybes, the ifs, the yeah buts—the

items you think you'll need someday. The kitchen and garage are good places to look. Remove anything that is just sitting there getting older and out-dated as time goes by.

These things can sometimes harm us—the old knives, the old lawn-mower, broken

glass, mousetraps. That table and chairs that only take up space, precious space.

Find a friend to help you take these items to the dump. When you return home do a

ceremony of release. Go to your altar, light as many candles as you feel drawn to, and offer thanks, first to your higher power, then to yourself, and to all those who helped

with this process.

Day 8

A Day of Banking

As long as you are in energetic debt, you will have banking debt. What do you bank on? Do you put all your energy into the future? Do you pray for more stuff, more things? "Once I have that BMW I will be at peace." Trust me, friend, the payment on stuff that subjugates us will never happen, and might help drive us to madness.

Do you lose energy when someone says something that upsets you? Do you steal from

your tomorrows by borrowing, thinking this will relieve your sorrows? When I opened the White Lilly in 2011, a clothing store created out of love for fashion, John and I had finally gotten ourselves out of debt. Within three years I put us in debt .

My energy debt began with the death of our child, the illness of my mother, the stroke

of my father. I also developed shingles twice that first year. I became very competitive, wanting more for the store instead of focusing on what was working. The clothing line, Goddess on the Go, was from Bali. New clothing stores began to open in our town —four within a year of my store's opening. I panicked, did not allow Spirit to have me, and began to spend more and more money purchasing for the White Lilly, thinking it would help business and take away my pain. I tell you this story to illustrate that we can begin to live unconsciously when stressed.

If you are losing energy, look at your bank account. Is it losing energy, too? Make a

commitment to yourself today to fill up that hole in your soul in other ways. If you are grieving, talk to someone who understands, someone who has experienced loss—not someone who has experience reading about loss from a book.

If you are lonely, go to a movie. Make a cake for someone and give it to them expecting NO THING in return. Visit a hospital and fill up your inner bank account with a day of service. Pay your bills, even if it is a little at a time. Ask your banker for help. Ask your higher self to remove any shame or pride you feel in reference to your debts. Eventually you will be out of debt, inside and out.

Day 9

A Day of Talent

Do you remember when you were younger, even before your twelfth birthday; you just

KNEW you had a talent? You did not name it "talent," but you felt a spark within you.

For me it was dancing. I would hear music and I was on fire. I danced every day, every moment when I found time alone. I would hear others comment to my mom or my friends about how wonderful my rhythm was. I had a teacher in grade eight who recommended I study dance.

When I dance I am one with the Divine, and I always KNEW this one thing. This talent came from God, so I would dance for God. I could feel God/Goddess flowing through my veins.

What is your talent? Don't over-analyze it. Try your best to remember. Was it drawing,

creating colors, singing, writing? Maybe it was throwing combinations of food together to make a feast.

Perhaps your mothering abilities came forth through babysitting. This is a talent; not everyone has the ability to mother, nurture, protect. Maybe it was a sport, and somewhere along the way you got carried away with life and put the baseball cap away.

Be with that talent today and bring it into being once again. It is the spirit of your

creative self having its way with you.

Day 10

A Day of Trust

This is your final day working with your mind—mind over matter. This is a day to

learn to rely on yourself. It is a day to trust your thoughts and your abilities. Do not doubt your brilliance. When you have a thought today that is creative—an idea about work or how to fix something—do not question it. Allow your thoughts to flow. Own them.

This is a day to celebrate all you have learnt about yourself thus far. You have learnt to

listen, to feel your surroundings, to be reasonable, to be responsible, to play, to laugh at

yourself. With confidence and self-esteem you will trust others. When you trust yourself,

you become more intuitive. You have begun to "let Spirit have you."

Ten Days Working with Your Body

Day 11

A Day of Breathing

Breathe. Inhale, taking oxygen into your lungs, and exhale. Sounds easy. We do it on
autopilot. But how many of us know how to breathe?
Upon waking today, lie where you are for a few extra minutes and observe how you
are breathing. Is it fast or shallow? Are you breathing fully into your lungs and slowly releasing, or is it quick-paced? When you feel agitated today, inhale deeply, filling your lungs, and then slowly let out the air. Feel how your agitation leaves your body with your breath. Every muscle relaxes. Your veins open. Your heart expands.
Imagine for a moment if a tree held its breath, or if a sparrow in flight held its breath. You only have so many days on this planet to enjoy the beauty of breathing. Why not be conscious of those moments? If you ever witness a loved one taking their last breath, you will appreciate each and every breath you bring into your being.

Day 12

A Day of Laughter

Sometimes we make others laugh because we want approval, we need to fit in, or we
are hiding from something. True laughter comes from the spirit within. It comes from the brain of our stomachs. It is like tiny bubbles bursting

in our bellies and tickling our hearts. It is the divine child in each of us expressing its true nature.

See the humour in everything you experience today. Even tragedy has a light. I remember when my brother took his own life in 2000. I had a dream that when he left his body he was surrounded by grey and his first words were, "Oh, shit. This dying is real." He started to laugh and said, "Oh well, now I can go on living without pain."

I awoke laughing because he was.

My mother was always laughing about something. She had glitter in her heart. Laughing

at our pain releases it. Not taking ourselves too seriously is one of the greatest gifts we give ourselves. It is also a wonderful gift to give to our children. With laughter we see with new eyes; we feel with new awareness. It's a short trip on this planet, so enjoy the joy of the ride.

Let's get over the seriousness of ourselves and get out from under our illusions. Humour

really is the best medicine.

Day 13

A Day of Drinking-in Life

Consume only fluids today. It's only a day—it will not harm you. Make a protein drink.

I love coconut water and almond milk. When doctors had no blood to use for patients during the First World War, they used coconut water for its nutrients. Drink water with a little lemon, ginger, cucumbers and mint—it's great for the digestive system. Stay away from sugared fruit drinks, pop, and coffee.

Water is our natural inheritance. Our bodies are fifty-five to seventy percent water. Pay attention to the quality of your drinking water, and drink this gift in. Pay attention to the quality

of the water you bathe in, and bathe consciously. Waste not the water you take for granted.

When you become more conscious of your day-to-day water consumption, you

become more of an activist in regard to the water supply on our planet.

Day 14

A Day of Eating Raw

Food. We love it, we hate it, we abuse it, we waste it.

Eat only raw food today. No, I am not talking about steak tartar. Fresh everything. Fruits, salads, and vegetables, to name a few. There are even raw chocolate cakes, pancakes, and much more. There are many recipes for eating raw available on the Internet. It is healthy and you will be in awe of how you feel, especially if you do this the day after drinking only fluids (Day 13).

Changing our eating habits can be very painful. For some it can be another loss.

Getting into good eating habits takes discipline, self-control, and inner power. At first it might feel awful, especially if you are an emotional eater – you feel raw. Slowly your body awakens from its dream of self-destruction and you feel alive.

Dr. Alejandro Junger's book *Clean* has become a way of life for me. (See www.cleanprogram.com.) No gluten, no dairy, no alcohol, no coffee, no sugar. My body, brain and spirit are clean, healthy and happy.

Day 15

A Day for a Walk

Do you remember what exercises you liked to do when you created the time? (Notice

I said created and not had the time.) We can all make time for ourselves when we are not sabotaging our moments. Find a walking buddy and chances are you will discover so much more about yourselves as you walkie/talkie. Don't want a walking buddy? That's okay. Just start walking. Fifteen minutes a day at first, and slowly work your way up to thirty minutes a day. Sneak away from work at lunchtime to walk. After dinner take a walk under the stars. If you are blessed to live by a beach, the walk will not only clear your mind and heal your body, but the waves will allow you to consciously flow to the rhythm of life.

If you are unable to travel, walking can take you into so many new territories. I often hear, "Walk your talk." Why? Just walk to your own dream. Words need not be said. You are never alone when you walk; Spirit is always with you, beside you, above you. All you have to do is breathe in the love and walk like no one is watching.

Day 16

A Day of Rest

Your health is never going to improve if you are running, working, caring for others,

mowing the lawn, watering the plants, and doing all the other chores that make up your day. Whether you are male or female, you need to rest. I hear women talk about how they nurture and take on so much, but I have known many a man who does the same.

There is nothing as refreshing as telling everyone you are taking a day off. This day off

can be spent in your bedroom or in a sacred place with just you and Spirit. No TV, no phone, no answering the door. If possible, be in your silence that we spoke of in Day 6. You will not only be resting your body but your mind as well. This rest will renew your cells, tickle your funny bone and give your immunity just what it needs.

It's a fresh outlook on the rest of your days to come.

Day 17

A Day of Habit

What is the one habit you want to let go of in your daily routines? Is it smoking? Drinking? Spending? Swearing? Needing to be right? Our habits appear in many forms and cause stress for our bodies. How about the habit of the TV, your iPhone,

your computer? Some of these habits can be life-threatening: smoking, drinking,

drugging.

Find someone you can trust, talk it out, see a professional, go to a twelve-step meeting.

You only have this day; what is the harm of attending one meeting? It might change your life. It did mine on October 7th, 1991.

"Just for today, I do not need another piece of stuff coming into this house." Leave the

TV off just for today. Put your iPhone away. You'll survive. It will be there tomorrow, and so will all your messages. Stay off Facebook today. Come face to face with habits that are making you sick and tired. Start a new habit. We talked about creating new habits in the first ten days. Start there.

Day 18

A Sugarless Day

"WHAT?!" you say. Sugar is fast becoming the number-one killer in our society. Sugar

is addictive and is a low-grade poison. Refined sugar provides only empty calories and has no nutrients. Our bodies do not know how to process the huge amounts of sugar we consume; it turns to fat.

Why do we want sugar? Simply because we are addicted to it. Ten years ago I took

sugar out of my diet for nine months. I was firm, healthy, glowing. We went on a cruise,

and one morning I ate some sugar, and by noon I was in tears. John asked me, "What

is the problem today?"

I had no idea (until later on). I responded, "I am leaking."

I am prone to addiction, so I have to stay off sugar. I manage by living one day at a time.

Don't eat anything that contains processed sugar today. Read the labels. FEEL how you feel tomorrow morning—no sugar hangover! Many of us have recurring headaches due to the effects of sugar but don't associate them with sugar.

Day 19

A Day without Gluten

Who does not love bread, pasta; anything made with flour that flowers the senses? For

years I suffered with mood swings, bloating, headaches. Our daughter Amanda has celiac disease. I am sure she was born with it, as she suffered with it throughout her childhood. I am convinced that our daughter Melanie, who took her own life in May of 2012, would still be alive if she had watched the gluten and sugar in her diet. My mother, Rosemary, in the same week was diagnosed with colon cancer. Coincidence? I think not. She lost her battle and died in October of 2013.

If we are what we eat, and the wheat is modified (see *Wheat Belly* by Dr. William Davis), then we are changing our very cells, and not for the good of our health. Try one day, today, with no gluten. My friend Kerry Ford has an informative Facebook page as well as her website, www.pan-andpanacea.com. She can help you with your holistic nutritional health. She can help you understand and create new eating habits.

Sweet Cheeks Kitchen is a gluten-free and vegan bakery right here in Almonte, Ontario, owned by mother and daughter Sharon and Kristen Lloyd. Here's their story, you might be able to relate. They also graciously shared two favourite recipes:

"Mom… I can't take the pain anymore."

There was no exclamatory in her remark, there was no plaintiveness, it was a simple phrase delivered with such resignation and despondency that it would make any mother's heart break.

That was the last straw! We had been to paediatricians, endured batteries of tests at our Children's Hospital and the last remark made to me by the specialists: "We can't find anything. Whatever it is, she'll outgrow it." We were then dismissed and on our own. The year was 1991 and my little girl was five.

Megs was born in 1986. She had been a very colicky baby, never sleeping. She

continually projectile vomited, endured diarrhoea or, alternately, constipation that left her bleeding from her rectum. We eventually were told to switch her to a soy formula. Shortly after, it was time to introduce her to toast fingers…whole wheat, of course, as I always tried to feed our children with a healthy and whole foods diet. Her symptoms were rampant! So went the following five years until that fateful day when she uttered the above words.

It was at this time that I decided that I was going to have to be very assertive with Megan's medical treatment. I approached our general practitioner, who was always open and helpful. I told her that I wanted to begin with a gastrointestinal specialist. Immediately upon the gastro specialist examining Megan, he said that she was not only lactose intolerant but allergic to the protein casein, as well. He told us it lurked in so many processed foods.

We became very proficient in finding milk ingredients in any and all foods. This definitely helped but it still wasn't the answer.

By process of deduction, we removed all wheat-based products. We still weren't

there! It required her being completely gluten free. After approximately two months, she was a new girl! We couldn't believe the difference…but our story doesn't stop here.

Her younger sister, Leah, had also been dairy-free from birth due to the same

allergy/intolerance. As the years progressed, Leah became more and more unwell. It manifested with severe brain fog, despondency, moodiness, and anxiety, which worsened in her teenage years. These were not the same symptoms as Megan's, yet they were all related to gluten sensitivity/intolerance. Leah became gluten free, as well, at this point.

It was several months later when we were driving down the road and she blurted out, "MOM, I CAN'T FEEL MY INTESTINES!!!"

My head snapped towards her… what did that mean??

She announced with triumph that she hadn't realized that she had been in such chronic pain and that she didn't know she could feel this way. There was no pain or discomfort in her abdomen, something she realized that had always been present.

Over the following months her mood improved dramatically. As well, the brain fog lifted and her look on life shifted dramatically.

Over the past two decades, living a gluten and dairy-free lifestyle, we found it very difficult for our girls to enjoy a treat along with everyone else. There were no coffee shops, cafes, or restaurants where they could enjoy a cup of tea with a dessert. The schools would have treats in the classroom or bake sales and our girls could not partake...only sit and watch the other children enjoy their treat. I cooked and baked all that I could at home and would pack little containers for the girls but inevitably the girls would find themselves in one of the above situations.

Three years ago, I left my full-time job to create a gluten-free and vegan kitchen and bakery with my oldest daughter. We felt very strongly that there needed to be easy access to quality gluten-free and vegan products. It was our local cafe that had the foresight to showcase our goods. It was only a few short months after we were supplying this local cafe, that I happened to be standing in line there, waiting to order a tea. The lady ahead of me took note of all of the different choices of gluten-free and vegan treats and voiced, "Finally, someone who

cares!" She didn't know that I was co-creator of her delights and I never said a word.

We still carry that phrase with us every day that we work in the kitchen. We really do care! We care about each customer that comes along with their special dietary needs. We now supply numerous cafes, restaurants, and grocery stores...providing easy access to high quality gluten-free and vegan goods that include both sweet and savoury. It is an absolute joy and honour to deliver a smile to all of those gluten-free girls and boys...and the big kids too, because let's face it, we're all still kids when it comes to a warm cookie!!

Recipe # 1: Quinoa Tabbouleh

1 cup quinoa

1 cup water

Rinse your quinoa for three minutes. Place in a pot with the water and bring to

a boil. Place lid on pot and cook over low heat for approximately 10 minutes or until the quinoa is light and fluffy. Remove from heat and let cool. (For quicker

cooling, place in the refrigerator.)

Dressing:

1/3 cup olive oil

2 tbsp fresh lemon juice

2 tbsp dried mint

1 tsp sea salt

dash of pepper

Whisk the above ingredients together and stir into the cooled quinoa. Add:

1 small bunch of finely chopped fresh parsley

3 green onions, finely chopped

1 tomato, coarsely chopped

Toss everything together and enjoy!

Recipe # 2: Carrot Cupcakes (makes 12)

1 1/2 c sugar

3/4 c oil

1 tsp vanilla

3 tbsp flax seeds

1/2 c non-dairy milk (soy or coconut work best)

2 1/2 c shredded carrot

1/4 c each chopped walnuts and drained pineapple tidbits

1 1/2 c of your favourite gluten-free flour mix

1 tsp baking soda

2 tsp cinnamon

2 pinches nutmeg

1 tsp xanthum gum

Preheat oven to 325 degrees F and place liners in cupcake tin. In a small bowl,

whisk flax and milk, and set aside. In a large mixing bowl add sugar, oil and

vanilla and beat with a hand mixer on medium to combine. Add flax mixture and carrots, and beat again on medium to combine very well. Add remaining

ingredients, mixing on low to combine until there are no lumps. Spoon equal

amounts (approx. a scant 1/4 cup) into the prepared cupcake tins.

Frosting:

1/4 c shortening

1/4 c vegan margarine

2 1/2 c icing sugar

zest of 1 lemon

1 tbsp lemon juice

non-dairy milk as needed

Beat ingredients 1-5 with hand mixer and dribble in non-dairy milk a teaspoon

at a time until a stiff but creamy consistency is made. Spoon into piping bag and

top the cooled carrot cuppies. Decorate with crushed walnuts and a drizzle of

brown rice syrup.

Day 20

A Day with Dr. Norm S*healy*

I first met Dr. Norm Shealy while studying with Caroline Myss in 2005. He is one

of the world's leading experts in pain and depression management. He was the first physician to specialize in the resolution of chronic pain. He developed Biogenics, the first comprehensive pain and stress management facility in the United States, which he founded in 1971. As he told us his story, we found out that in 1978 he was instrumental in developing the American Holistic Medical Association. He is also the founder of the National Institute of Holistic Medicine.

I was very excited about his information on essential oil blends, which can effectively

stimulate the circuits that enhance dehydroepiandrosterone (DHEA). DHEA is a hormone that is naturally made by the human body.

From Wikipedia: "It can be made in the laboratory from chemicals found in wild yam and soy. However, the human body cannot make DHEA from these chemicals, so simply eating wild yam or soy will not increase DHEA levels. DHEA is used for slowing or reversing aging, improving thinking skills in older people, and slowing the progress of Alzheimer's disease."

Dr. Shealy's Air Bliss provides calmness and relief from depression and anxiety. He teaches about the acupuncture circuits that help balance our elemental energies and how applying his oils affects these circuits. The Bliss oil categories are: Air, Crystal, Earth, Fire, and Water. Each bottle is 1/3 oz. A bottle of Bliss comes with corresponding information and instructions. Go to www.NormShealy.com. Start today with Bliss oils—I wouldn't be without them.

Ten Days Working with Your Spirit

You've had ten days with your mind, ten days with your body, and now we come to my favourite; ten days working with your spirit. The whole of you. The holy you.

I start my day with my mantra: "Just for today, let Spirit have me." I began a few years

ago after studying with Caroline Myss. She has a love of Saint Teresa of Avila. I was smitten with a sculpture by Gian Lorenzo Bernini, which he created during the years 1647-52. It is called the Ecstasy of Saint Teresa. It looks to me like Saint Teresa is in total union with Spirit—the deep giving of herself, letting Spirit have her.

Day 21

A Day of Letting Spirit Have You.

Upon waking, or just before you drift into the ethers the night before, make a

commitment to listen only with your heart today. Listen to what feels right, not what you think might be the best start to your day. Follow your feelings, your bliss. Yes, yes, I know the kids are screaming, the car won't start, the rent is due, and funds are low. Pretend just for today that everything is in divine order. Imagine that you are receiving help from an outside source—a spirit that is leading you and guiding you through this difficult day. Try not to question. Be like a child. Believe in the power of prayer. If you can, start a soul companion prayer group that meets once a month.

There will be days when you are so drained you cannot pray or talk to God/Goddess,

so have someone else pray for you. Develop a prayer community in unity within your

community to nurture mind, body, and spirit. Don't we all aspire to finding peace in chaos? Sometimes we need each other to help us along the journey.

Day 22

A Day of Prayer

Speaking of prayer, I pray all day long. I talk to God/Goddess. I speak with the spirits

of those who have recently passed, the spirits of those to come, and of course our ancestors from long ago. I don't ask for much, really—peace, a day free from stress, good health and the health of all I hold dear. When I cannot pray because I have allowed fear to enter and I am in survivor's mode, I put out an NPN (Need Prayers Now) to my many friends. I ask that they light a candle and pray that I, my family, and anyone needing courage and strength accept whatever outcome Spirit has for us.

Prayer is the grace we are given. Use it. Miracles happen. Pray today. Talk to God/

Goddess, Universal Source. Know you are never alone.

> "Dear God/Goddess/Universal Source, today may I see myself in your likeness, no matter how beautiful or wonderful I am."

> "Dear God/Goddess/Universal Source, thank you, thank you, thank you. Yes, yes, yes."

> "Dear God/Goddess/Universal Source, I believe that anything is possible because everything is possible with your help and guidance."

> "Dear God/Goddess/Universal Source, I am open to receive my assignment for this day. Whatever task is set before me I accept with joy."

"Dear Friend, I am working on all of your problems. Now stay out of my way.

Your friend, God/Goddess/Universal Source."

A few years ago a friend mentioned to me that she did not like saying some of our
Catholic prayers; one in particular—the Act of Contrition. Telling or praying to a God who she felt was going to judge her was not her gig. She felt like she was praying to a domineering father figure she had to confess to.

How can we change our perspective of the wording in a prayer to tell our story? When
I say, "My God, I am heartily sorry for offending thee," I am talking to Gaia, the living earth, and the collective. Have I been attentive, conscious of what is going on with our planet? I am talking to the kingdom that also lives inside me. Spirit gave us free will.

"Thy will be done on Earth as it is in Heaven." Think about those words. I walk on
Earth but Heaven resides in and around, above and beyond me. When I say the Our Father, I am talking to the universal source that bonds us. When I repeat the Hail Mary, I am loving and affirming the Divine Goddess/feminine energy in each of us. I am blessing all that is, has been, and will be.

What if we change our perspective—not the words of the prayers but how we feel about them? It can be a religious prayer, a poem, a word or a devotion. Prayers have been with us for centuries; they must have some power. What if your life changed because of your PRAYERS? Just for today let the power of prayer have you.

Day 23

A Day of Forgiveness

Oh dear, this will be a big day for you. Forgiveness is just another word for freedom.

When we forgive either ourselves or others we allow our hearts to burst open and we begin to bloom. Like the lily that closes up at night in the shadow, once a day, it breaks open into its own beauty. Such are you when you open to the light within. You will know and feel your own beauty.

Forgiveness comes in many forms. The forgiveness for myself and how I treated our

daughter Melanie is in a poem called "Reflections of a Shadow Self" in my book of

poems, *Lilly White Lies & Dreams.*

At first forgiveness feels brittle—the "No, never again." But at the end of your day

— at the end of your days—will it matter? What matters is love. Nothing else. You will want to tell your side of the story, but remember that the one you are forgiving has his or her interpretation of that story.

Own your story, relive it if you must, then let it go. Change your story. See the symbolism in what happened or is happening. Learn to say, "I am sorry." They may forgive you or they may not; your intent is love. That is your story for today. Now, doesn't forgiveness feel freeing?

As Kris Kristofferson and Fred Foster said in the song "Me and Bobby McGee,"

"Freedom's just another word for nothing left to lose." You have nothing left to lose, but everything to inherit and gain. Your stairway to Heaven is accessible now.

You are free.

Day 24

A Day with Angels

I have felt angels, spirits, the unknown energy above and below me since I was five. It

seems like yesterday to me. As I got older I forgot they were with me except during those times when I experienced the death of a friend or loved one.

When I was in my late thirties, I experienced them once again with great passion. I heard their urgency to talk. They talked to me in the morning, during meditation, at night during prayer, and at the gym. The angel Paul was always there when I was cooking. They talked so much that I decided to study them and understand their messages.

I travelled to Laguna Beach, California and through Doreen Virtue become a certified angel therapist practitioner. That is when I discovered the beauty of angel cards and how to read and interpret them. That was a long time ago, and since then we have evolved into higher-frequency-of-light beings. Consider buying a pack of angel cards , get to know who the angels are and what their symbolism means. Start your own daily readings.

Angels are messengers of light, messengers of love, messengers of God/Goddess.

YOU are that light. These energies are within you, above you, below you, and next to you.

Day 25

A Day with Your Archetypes
"How can you help and know others if you do not know yourself?"
Caroline Myss

I believe that learning about Caroline Myss's sacred contracts and your twelve archetypes will bring you into an awareness of self that no one else can give you. You can seek all you want and study as many modalities as you can afford to, but you always come back to KNOWING THYSELF.

Pick up a copy today of *Sacred Contracts: Awakening Your Divine Potential* by Caroline Myss, and find her archetype cards. If funds are short, your librarian might be able to help you borrow a set of cards, or you can get creative and make your own after you've studied her book, or put them on your wish list and do the work required to manifest them. Your intent is for the highest good, so do not be afraid—be aware. They will show up in your life once you synchronize with your highest potential.

Day 26

A Day with Soul Companions
Look into starting a soul group today. In 2006 I founded a group called Breakfast With Soul. We got together the last Friday of each month until I opened my store in 2010. From that group came the Power Up Your Life weekend with Dr. Mona Lisa Schultz in 2009 and with Andrew Harvey in 2011.

Don't be surprised when you draw people who are looking into their souls and finding

their spirits. People are shy to open up at first, but if you speak your truth, so will they. When I began, I would sit with a cup of coffee in a coffee shop called Groundz, in Almonte, Ontario. Within a few months there were twenty-two on our Breakfast With Soul list, and ten or twelve showed up consistently for breakfast. Bonds were made that will last our lifetimes. As Desmond Tutu said at Quest for Global Healing in Bali in 2005, "You are all God Creators. Now go create God."

Day 27

A Day of Travel

In astrology, the ninth house is the house of spirituality and long-distance travel.

Travelling has allowed me to get closer to the universal source that I call God/Goddess. I have had opportunities to grow at a deep level, especially during my yearly trips to Bali since 2003.

I realize that not everyone is able to travel, but we have the web (the inner net!) We can fill ourselves up daily with stories of other countries and their cultures, their religions, their beliefs. No matter how far you travel or how many miles you cross on Google Maps, we are all fundamentally the same. Our desires are the same. We all have God, our families, our health, our work, and our worries, though many of us are blessed because of the country we live in. We all seek love, to be loved and to be loving.

Think about curtailing some of your spending on things that don't further your horizons today—tobacco, drugs, booze, and more clothing and gadgets than you need—and save a little for travel. It can be to another province or state or across the park to a new neighbourhood. Go where your heart directs. Return with many blessings and remember to bless those you meet.

Day 28

A Day of Feeling Worthy

Do you ever feel unworthy?

I had a dream recently that I was in church with a special friend, Jill Angelo.

Caroline Myss was teaching us about love. In front of me, someone dropped two amulets on the floor and I thought they were for someone else. Two men appeared through the side door and one reached down and passed the amulets to me. I realized that the man was Jesus, and the other man was Michael, and I was shocked that Jesus thought I was good enough to receive the amulets. He simply said, "They were always yours." Then Jesus and Michael left.

I asked Caroline why I still felt unworthy after so many years of training, and she said, "Lilly, it's still all in your head. It's not about what your father did, or your schooling, it's about your seeing yourself as Jesus sees you. You are loved because you exist. Go into your sacred heart."

I understood the message of this dream: I am to embrace what God and others have given me—unconditional love, acceptance, and trust. When I feel these I am filled with Grace. I am blessed.

See yourself as God sees you today—how the universe absorbs you, how your loved

ones feel you. You will have more blessings bestowed on you than you can ever imagine or pray for.

Say, "I am worthy. I am worthy to receive."

Day 29

A Day of Opening a Door

Open your door to whoever knocks today—not just the door to your dwelling, but to the

house of your heart; your soul. Be open to all possibilities. Let go of any fear and stop saying NO to everything. Learn to say YES, YES, YES. Thank you, thank you, thank you.

Do you give, or always take?
Is the shadow of your beggar still awake?
Can you freely give your time, money, space?
If your answer is no, you will meet yourself, face to face.
Is your life working you, or are you falling apart?
Do you never finish that which you start?
Are you repeating a pattern and blaming the other?
Chances are the problem isn't your mother.
Is the shadow of your saboteur alive and well?
Witnessing yourself is how you will tell.
Are you able to let go and breathe yourself in?
It is within this space you will begin
To BE your divine self.
Your victim shattered, it did not win.
Your highest potential beckons,
Can you hear its call?
It says, "I live inside you,
Trust yourself, you have it all."

Day 30

A Day of Service

"Go now and do."

Help where you are needed, with no expectations in return. Babysit, cook for someone, walk a dog for a neighbour, call someone who is sick. Help someone buy food for his or her table. You do not have to move a mountain to be of service. Move love around, dance it inward, pay it forward—whatever it takes. Service is not what we DE-SERVE, it is how we best SERVE. Get out of ME. We are now in the consciousness of WE.

At this time in our evolution we are being called and urged to expand our vision. The
secret is getting over ourselves and learning to see others first and ourselves second. Only then will we develop tools to rise above the five senses and tune in to our sixth sense; able to feel what our eyes do not see in the third dimension.

We have become obsessed with I: "I need to look after my feelings, my space, my thoughts." This comes from our intellects. When we move from our intellects we make room for living from our hearts. We stop the fight with I.

To be able to step out of your pain, feel the pain of your friend, partner, parent, or child; and do something about it. This is what I believe Jesus was teaching us symbolically when he died on the cross. It was never about him; it was about humanity. "Forgive them, they know not what they do."

I don't want you to let someone walk over your boundaries, but to step out of your personal pain and think of the other first. Hurt people hurt people. If someone is hurting you in some way, it is because that person is hurting. Can you step aside today and love them the way they are, unable to love themselves?

If you are living consciously and walking your talk, then yes, you will feel the pain, yet by stepping into the light you will focus on the other person without judgment. I realize from my own experience that this is not always easy. I have days, hours, minutes when I have to repeat to myself, "Focus on this person's needs."

Allow Spirit to have you. Whether it involves another's business, family, livelihood or self-esteem, because they are loved by you they will start thinking of others instead of themselves and pass it on. Passing love on is where YOU and ME become THEE.

We are past the shadow energy of hurting ourselves by denying others love. Repeat to yourself, "JUST FOR TODAY… LET SPIRIT HAVE ME."

Day 31

Your Day Off

If this month has thirty-one days, relax! This is your day to play and forget everything else. Take the day off and have fun!

30-Day Challenge Workbook

YOU DID IT! You finished the 30-Day Challenge. Now start again from the beginning

so these messages become a part of you. There will be days you will say no. It is always easier to go backward than it is to go forward; backward is familiar territory. It is the unknown that scares us because we have no control over it.

Be aware, be not afraid.

You are not alone as you Power Up Your Life.

These tools are yours. Live them, use them, and give them away. They came from

Spirit—always the spirit of YOU. We are after all a collective, in unity within our community to nurture our minds, bodies and spirits.

Just for today… let Spirit have you!

Dear God/ Goddess.

May we have faith in the thunderstorm. May we accept that depression is not a personal thing, it is a collective—we all suffer in ways unknown to others. May we be brave enough to reach out and ask for more help, time and time again. May we KNOW that if I am de com pressing today someone is holding my Joy. That is all we need; each other to pray and play together.

Thank God/Goddess,
Amen

The END of sorrow for a blessed tomorrow.

The Final Chapter

God, are you kidding me?

It is Saturday, Midnight, August 13, 2016. I have just flown into Calgary from Ottawa. The fight arrives at 9:30pm and I arrive at midnight to Bethany home where our dad is living since our mothers death two years ago.

We had arrived home to Almonte, just outside Ottawa from Newfoundland the previous Friday, a day before and the next day I am in the air. Give me a break. Seeing and being with Melanie's children was happy but I was filled with grief when we said our goodbye's. Now you want me to what? Say good-bye to my Daddy'o. Never, no, not.

Jesus, are you listening? I do not have the strength for this. Ask John, my mate for the last 43 years. He almost left me when I was lamenting our Grandchildren a few days ago. Now you are requesting I pull out my soul, put away my ego and let you have me again and again. Just a minute. I need time. Jesus are you nuts or am I once again into Madness.

Suddenly, I hear a voice; I have entered Dad's room, room 229. I know it by heart. Since Mom's death, I have been blessed to visit every three months. Like clockwork.

Oh yes, the voice. "Go lie down with your father". "I can't there is not enough room"

"Go lie down, I will make room." ..Jesus is this you cause if not, this is crazy making. "Never mind your mind, go with your heart, and lie down, NOW"

I make my way to Dad's bed and see a railing and put it up. I climb on the right side of the bed and find that I am very comfortable as I put my arm around his shoulder and stroke his face and then his heart. He is unable to response but the smile on his face tells me he is comfortable and aware someone is there. My voice sounds like Mom so perhaps he thinks it is her.

The next morning the doctor arrives and says he is worse than yesterday. No fluids. He explains that Dad had made the decision to die in the home rather than hospital. Wise Daddy'o. I however am alarmed as there is no IV or fluids. In a home such as Bethany, this is what happens. No hospital equipment to keep patients alive. It is Dad's choice and I am in sorrow. He is leaving, on his own terms.

Our family is together this day, Kenny, Kathy, Deborah and myself, all that is missing is our brother Al. Derek another brother left us in 2000. He took his life and is now waiting for our Dad. To show him the reason he left. with non-judgment.

We have good nights sleep. I do not leave his side.

Monday morning, Dad looks like he is about to leave and I ask him to wake up. I try and give him water, I say" Daddy O wake up, wake up "From deep, deep below he says, and I can hardly hear, " I can't". I respect that, wet his lips and leave him alone for the day. To sleep.

During the day people are coming and going. My sisters Deb and Kathy are with me as well and Derek's son James and his bride to be.

We laugh and model cloths from Stella's. A fashion boutique our Mom used to work at. Fashions on Main. Stella is like a sister and she knows what will tickle us, the fashionista's. We have a fashion show in Dad's room and although others will think this blasphemy and uncouth, we know Dad is listening and enjoying that we feel at home. Why change who we are. He would not have wanted us to. He loved that we knew style and lived it. As our Mother, his beloved Rosemary.

I leave his room for an hour to shower and change; I have not done this since Saturday. I am tired but alert to my Daddy'o.

Tuesday, I awake next to Dad. He has had a peaceful sleep. Deborah arrives with John, who has just flown in. Dad is not responding. Trying to put liquids into him is at a loss. Adding moisture to his lips is all we can do. I leave once again to shower and get John comfortable at our friend Myra's home.

We pick up food for those who are visiting us while we are in Dad's room.

John and I arrive at 2:30 and I suggest to Deb that perhaps we eat in the kitchen. "No," she reply's, something tells me to stay with Dad. I concur. John leaves while her and I eat a salad and sandwich. At 3:10 our Dad opens his eyes and the bed shakes. He is awake after all this time. We approach but he does not look good. I tell him he is going to be OK.

I am to the right of him, Deborah to the left. He stares into my eyes with his baby blues and I KNOW this is it. He is leaving. (Don't cry, don't break down, rock him through this), I say to self.

I tell him how much we all love him, I name all his children one by one and with each name he takes a deeper breath. I tell him his mommy is waiting first in line to greet him. Her name was Lillian (Lilly) He has not seen her since he was 18 months old. She was only 26 yrs. when she died of TB in 1936. (Dad never got over the pain of that, hence his anger, madness, addictions). He smiles. I tell him that our mother, his wife is waiting, his granddaughter, our daughter and of course his son, our brother, Derek. They are all anxiously awaiting him. I am helping him give birth to his soul, I tell him this. He continues to look at me. I suggest to Deb to keep massaging his heart as she so loves doing, and he looks at her. I then tell him that our brother Al is on his way from Nepal. My words are," Dad, Al loves you so much he is on his way to see you and say goodbye. But Dad your body is giving out, it's been a long journey for your body and its time to let go. AL will be here soon. Your body is sick but your soul is being rebirthed to others that love you also. "He looks at Deborah and takes his last breath. It is 3:30pm, August 16th, 2016. Alberta time.

Deb and I grieve alone before we go alert the staff.

We ask them not to touch his body until our brother arrives so Dad looks like he is asleep. Al arrives at midnight and says his own goodbyes.

The next day, we, the family are together and clean out Dad's room. Arrangements and goodbyes are scheduled for Friday the 19th.

August the 19th, it is a beautiful day and Dad and his bride are now together in harmony.

Although our parents are no longer with us there is a deep connection between siblings and for that I am humbled and in deep gratitude.

A new chapter has begun. Freedom, choices, acceptance. We are now the elders.

My last visit to Dad when he was coherent and happy was May 2016. I was hosting a workshop with friends.. On my last day with him, just before I flew out, a nurse came in and he introduced me as his daughter, the author. He had never done this before so I was startled. The nurse asked me about my first book "365 ways to Power Up Your Life", I mentioned I had just finished my second book, "Madness, Addiction & Love".

She asked a few questions, we chatted and when she left my dad was in his bed turned to the right of me and asked, "What side of the family do you think this mental illness comes from?" I was shocked at his question. We never discussed mental illness, as I was afraid he would take it personally and not understand what is really going on. The addictions, our food, our DNA etc.

My reply was, "from both sides". He looked at me and went to sleep. I am sure he wanted to say, F off.

In closing, you have read about him, our daughter and myself. Our addictions, our madness but more importantly, our love.

No matter what, Love is the only answer. No matter what happens, what we are fated for in this lifetime, love is the Holy Grail, our destiny. But to love we need to know ourselves. We need to accept our heritage, our lineage, our DNA. We do this with non-judgment, acceptance & grace. We need to pray and play.

"WE LET SPIRIT HAVE US"

Acknowledgements

Without my mother and father this book would have no beginning. They did their best, they loved us the only way they knew in the way they were accustomed, and I will love them forever.

To John, my EGO buster, you keep me grounded.

Our children—my greatest teachers. Sometimes I was not the best student. It took time for me to understand.

Our grandchildren, Breanna, Madeleine, Xavier, Carter, Tatiana, and Zofia. You gave me love with no strings, no conditions and during the writing of this, the days when I wanted to throw it all away, you reminded me of why I was putting myself and our lives out there—to help and serve others in love. Unconditional love.

To our friends, Susan Prosser, Suzanne Win-Love Smith, Linda Rawn, Paddy Doyle, Julie, Michele T, Diana Boal, Carole Dallaire, Louise B and Louise BS, Myra, Rene, Gloria Benjamin, Rose Ford, Sherry, Rona Fraser, Christine, Wendy, Rondi, Elaine Luedey, Suzanne Kennedy, Bonnie Pike, Brenda Needman and Lynn Mayer—thank you for your support while I was writing this book.

To the five lights; Mary, Ruth Anne, Margaret, Georgia, and Deborah. May you always shine in compassion, unity, love, peace and joy. May Archangel Uriel always lead us further into light and truth.

To Facebook friends who took the time to read "Peeks for Peeps," thank you for your encouragement. I am always in awe of your love and acceptance.

To our friends in Bali; Agung Prana, Hai Dai, Agung Wah, Made, Dewa, Janet O'Malley from Goddess on the Go, and so many more of you—thank you for showing me what love is.

> *It's seven in the morning*
> *I am still mourning the breeze of the Bali Sea.*
> *I awake to crystals on windowsills*
> *that whispers their magic to me.*
> *"The air that you breathed from the Bali Sea has followed you home.*
> *settled in clouds and fall lovingly for you to see.*
> *We are with you in spirit wherever you roam."*

To God/Goddess: Thank you for allowing me to co-create with you. For showing and leading me into thyself. I love you. I love that I am mad, addictive, and in love. Without the parents I had, the marriage I chose, and the decisions I made, I would not be who I am. The light and shadow of these decisions is what helped me become conscious and brave, and to graduate into my truth.

"Just for today, le the spirit of Truth have you."

THE REST OF ME

When my last breath of delight is in the universe

When my eyes close to enter the cosmos

Free me to the breeze of Bali to the shores of home

For there you will find me.

Our Father

Who art in Heaven, hallowed be thy name, thy kingdom come, thy will be done, on Earth as it is in Heaven.

We are the kingdom; the universe, lives inside us.

Give us this day our daily bread, forgive us our trespasses as we forgive those who trespass us and deliver us from evil, amen.

Eat only what your body requires for today. Forgive yourself; forgive others; discipline yourself through your self will; will yourself to not be temped to dishonour your body, your mind, and your spirit.

Know thyself

Forgive

Eat healthy

Follow discipline

Just for today, let the spirit of the prayer "Our Father" have you.

Now is not the time to be afraid—be aware. We stand in unison as a collective. We stand in love and courage and will soldier on, no matter what is thrown at us. This is our world. This chaos is happening everywhere, in our mind/bodies, in our homes, our towns, our counties, our planet. Breathe, continue to be in your light, pass that light on and together we will brighten the darkness.

"For today, let the spirit of light have us." What does that mean? Allow your attention to be in prayer. Pray all day long if you have to. That does not mean we need to be in meditation, on our knees, or in a church. Your mind/body is your church. If you choose to be on your knees, go for it. Continue to be in gratitude, for the small things; the sun, your children, your health, your day. You are alive at this moment. Make the most of it. All is in Divine order. Difficult to believe I realize but nothing is random. Your prayers do make a difference; it is part of your sacred contract. Remember what you came here for. Do not allow the darkness to shadow your light. Be YOU.

Love like there is no tomorrow,
Love like you have never experienced sorrow
Love as the trees need the breeze to cool off their leaves.

Love as a newborn needing their mommy to feed.
Love as your first kiss, the tenderness, the moisture, as deep as the mist,
LOVE, LOVE, LOVE
"Just for today, Let the SPIRIT of LOVE have YOU."

Lilly is also author of 365 Ways to Power Up Your Life

(tools for intuitive living)

Soon to be released

Bali Coffee, Cloves Cigarettes & Fairy Travels

Her website is www.lillywhite.ca

CPSIA information can be obtained
at www.ICGtesting.com
Printed in the USA
LVHW110817070822
725352LV00013BA/167/J